How to Boost Your Church Attendance

by
DR. JACK HYLES

REPRINTED AND PUBLISHED
BY
HYLES PUBLICATIONS
Hammond, Indiana
for the 38th annual Pastors' School
March 19–22, 2001
First Baptist Church, Hammond, Indiana

In memory of Dr. Jack Hyles
September 25, 1926 – February 6, 2001

HOW TO BOOST YOUR CHURCH ATTENDANCE
First printed in 1958
Eighteenth printing of original manuscript–
Memorial Edition for Pastors' School 2001

Printed in the United States of America

Dedicated to my wife,
BEVERLY,
*who has shared with me in the successes
and failures, joys and heartaches, in
the learning and using of the
material contained in
this book.*

PREFACE

In December, 1952, I was called to become pastor of the Miller Road Baptist Church in Garland, Texas, a church with an annual budget of $3,000 and ninety-two members. The church had property valued at $6,000. In the five years of our fellowship and work together God has seen fit to increase those figures to over 3,400 members, a budget of $182,000 annually, and property evaluated at $500,000.

During those years many pastors have come to me wanting to know about our methods and ideas concerning the church program. After four years of these inquiries and conferences, we conducted in our church a pastors' school. At the conclusion of the pastors' school the brethren suggested that the information and data be compiled in book form. This book was written from the notes that were presented in the pastors' school.

Many churches, especially small ones, have used the ideas presented in this book to great benefit. No one pastor will agree with all of the ideas suggested. Neither will all of the ideas work in all situations; however, it is hoped that from the suggestions a few points may be applicable to each minister, and that some suggestions will be helpful to each church.

May the God of heaven bless these promotional ideas and suggestions to the bringing of souls to our Saviour.

JACK HYLES

CONTENTS

1. Practical Pointers for the Pastor and His People

One of the most disheartening things in the modern church is the seeming disharmony between many pastors and their people. I believe that one of the most sacred relationships in all of the world is the relationship that the pastor of a church should have with his people. God is not pleased when the people are dissatisfied with the pastor. Neither is God pleased when the pastor has a bitter attitude toward his people. God wants the pastor and the people to love each other, to pray together, work together, serve together, worship together, win souls together, give together. Following are some suggestions that will help the pastor understand his people.

1. *Love Your People.* Ask God to give you a heart full of love for the people you serve. This does not mean that you can always condone what they do. Many times a parent who loves his child will have to spank him hard, and the child may doubt the parent's love; however, behind the heart of a true parent there is a love that realizes it is best for the child to receive punishment for his errors. This is also true with a pastor. A pastor who scolds his people because he is tired of their sinning, is wrong. A pastor whose heart is broken because of the sins of his people, and scolds them for their own good, is right. Many evangelical ministers have failed in this respect because of the lack of a deep, abiding love for their people.

2. *Be Expressive in Your Love for Your People.* Some preachers carry a little pad around with them, and a pencil, and when they think of some member who has been a blessing to them, they jot the name down and later

write the member a note or express appreciation personally to one who has been a blessing. Our people do
much for us — they pray for us, overlook our faults, forget our mistakes and make us what we are. Let us express to them our love and appreciation.

3. *Pray for Your People.* The pastor should call the
names of his people in prayer, especially those who have
burdens and heartaches. When a home is having trouble,
the pastor should pray for them. When Johnny has the
measles, or Mary has the mumps, the pastor should pray
for them. Many times a little note to Johnny will be an
encouragement to him; or a phone call to Mary might
be a blessing. It is always good for a pastor to pray for
his people.

4. *Do not Use Your People to Build a Great Work, But
Use Your Work to Build Great People.* Some have the
idea that it is the job of the preacher to build churches.
This is not true. It is the job of the preacher to build
people to be great Christians. To use the people to build
a work is wrong; to use the work to build great people
is right. The greatest product of a pastor is a steadfast
Christian, and not a sanctuary. The greatest work of
a pastor is to see a Christian grow in the grace of the
Lord, and not to see the membership grow. Individuals
are important. When a preacher can see his people individually and rejoice more over a Christian who grows
than over a building that goes up, then he has developed
a true pastor's heart.

To use our people as stepping stones for our ministry
is not fair; neither is it Christlike.

5. *Make Your People Feel That You Are Theirs.* People
like to feel as if they have a pastor. They like to feel
as if the pastor belongs to them, and that they belong
to him. Do not let your people feel secondary. Spend
your time with them. Many preachers spend so much time
with each other that their people feel they cannot have
fellowship with their pastor. Live with your people, love
them, pray for them, work with them and seek their
good — not your own.

6. *Eat in the Homes of Your People.* It is good for the pastor to be in the homes of the people. When your people invite you for a meal, try never to reject such an invitation. It is a mutual blessing. The people need the fellowship with the pastor; the pastor needs the fellowship of the people. Children know the pastor better when he comes into their homes. If he is kind, thoughtful and understanding to the children, they will become his pals, and will feel that he belongs to them.

7. *Give the People Some Time at Home.* Many of our people are tired. We preach to them hard and long that they should have a Christian home, and then give them no time to have a Christian home. A preacher should encourage his people to spend some time at home. Then, he should not plan such a heavy church program that it will take all of their nights, so that they do not have the opportunity to have a Christian home. It is difficult to come in at midnight with sleepy children and have a family altar. However, with some nights at home together with the family, it becomes easier to pray together and stay together. When the families realize that the preacher is concerned about their problems, then they will love and appreciate him more.

8. *Be with Them in Hours of Need.* When a person is to have an operation, go to the hospital and have a period of prayer with him. When a couple is married, spend some time with them. When a baby comes, rejoice over the coming of the baby. It has long been my conviction that the pastor should not receive remuneration for the things he does for his members. It seems to me that marrying the church members is a part of the pastor's duties; hence, it would seem inadvisable to accept a fee for marrying one of my church members. Little things like these make a pastor dear to the hearts of his people. Of course, it should not be our desire or our aim to become dear to the hearts of the people. These things should come naturally to the true man of God who loves his people.

9. *Remember That Your People Make You What You*

Are. A good church can make a good preacher; a poor church can make a poor preacher. All that we are, we have been made by the Lord, and God has used our dear people to make us what we are. Many times people come to me at Miller Road Church and say, "Pastor, God has used you to make me what I am." Then, I go home and think — God has used my church to make me what I am. Our soul winners, and those who pray and are faithful, have helped to make our church what it is. Because of that, the pastor has opportunities open to him that he would not have had, had the people not worked for the Lord Jesus. Never forget, dear pastor friend, that what you are is largely a work of Christ as He has used your people to make you what you are.

10. *Never Reject Anything From Your People.* Dr. Truett used to say, "Even if all they offer you is a glass of water, drink it. They are offering it as unto the Lord." You are God's man, and they are offering you something as God's man; hence, never reject it. Accept it, and be grateful to God, regardless of how small the gift.

2. How to Get People to Visit

The problem in every church seems to center around visitation. Other pastors are constantly asking me, "How do you get your people to visit?" "How can you get folks on the field?" They are always trying to find new methods and new ways to encourage people to visit for Jesus. Following are some suggestions for the pastor on this subject.

1. *Make Every Service Evangelistic.* If people go out to win souls to Christ, and bring lost people to a service in which there is not a spirit of evangelism, those who visit will be discouraged. It is the pastor's job to be sure that the services are evangelistic and not disappointing. Many times people will visit, bring a lost person to the service and then the pastor preaches a sermon on budget-raising or some other similar subject and the lost person has no conviction whatsoever. Someone has said that when Jesus wanted some money to pay His taxes, He found the money in the fish's mouth. It seems that it would be wise for us to spend our time getting fish. When they are caught and converted, then the money will be in their mouths.

To say the least, every service should end with an evangelistic appeal to let the sinner know that others are concerned about him, and to let the soul winner know that any time he brings a lost person to the services, there will be a sincere appeal made for his salvation.

2. *Visit and Let the People Know It.* Each pastor and each leader of the church should be a personal soul winner. If you are not a soul winner, you cannot train

your people to be soul winners. If you do not visit regularly, you cannot train your people to visit regularly. Be sure that your people are conscious of the fact that you are a perennial visitor and soul winner. To be such a person will be exceedingly difficult. The devil will block you at every hand to discourage your regular visitation program. I would suggest that as a pastor or special worker you set aside at least two days each week in which you do nothing but visit prospects, and let nothing except an emergency hinder your visitation program. When your people know that you are a fervent, consistent soul winner, then you will be leading them and not pushing them.

3. *Make Visitation Seem the Most Important Thing in the Church.* Many people think that being a deacon is more important than being a soul winner. That is not true. Many people think that being a Sunday school or youth worker is more important than being a soul winner. That is not true, either. The greatest job in the world is the job of bringing people to Christ. If the pastor will magnify the job of soul winning above the other jobs of seeming importance in the church, then the people will get the idea that soul winning is the most important thing in the church.

4. *Choose Your Teachers from Those Who Visit.* Show your people that you believe soul winning is important by selecting your teachers and officers from those who visit regularly. This will encourage visitation on the part of those who are not teachers.

5. *Do Not Work People on "Odds and Ends" Too Much.* Many people are so busy working around the church doing such jobs as carpenter work or decorating, that they feel this is their service for God. I realize that many churches must be built by the members, and that is well and good. It is always good for a plumber to use his profession and talent at the church. It is good for carpenters and electricians to use their talents at the church —but keep before the people the fact that this is not their complete service for Christ. Keep reminding them

that Christ expects them to be soul winners and witnesses apart from their other work at the church. Many of us have taught our people the wrong interpretation of the parable of the talents. We say that if all you can do is shake hands at the door, then do it the best you can. Or, if all that you can do is put flowers in the vase, do it the best you can. Dear friend, when Jesus gave us the commission to go into all the world and teach all nations, He was giving it to each of us. Every Christian should be a witness. Certainly we should use our talents at the church, yet the commission is still true. Each of God's people is to be a soul winner. Let us not discourage our people from doing the *main* thing by encouraging them too much in doing other things.

6. *Have a Soul Winning and Visitation Course Annually.* At least once each year in our church we have a course on soul winning and visitation, teaching our people how to win souls to Christ in a simple, straightforward way. This should be done, I believe, from the Bible, with no other textbook, unless it is used only as a supplement.

After the first year you will need to provide two courses—one for advanced soul winners and one for beginners. We have made it a practice not to worry about awards at the end of the course. The greatest award or examination that one could ever receive or pass would be to see someone converted through his efforts. The examination is on the battlefield for God, and the awards will be given at the Judgment Seat.

Make this a practical study course in soul winning. A following chapter will be given to soul winning, and will be a good chapter to consult in teaching the course.

7. *Get Committals on Wednesday Night.* Our visitation program is on Thursday. Since it is, we encourage our people at the midweek service on Wednesday night to come to visitation on Thursday. Many times we stress it more than at other times by asking the people to raise their hands or stand, and promise to come. If they will commit themselves on Wednesday night, usually they will come on Thursday night.

If your visitation is on Monday or Tuesday, then perhaps a committal on Sunday night would be in order.

8. *Do Not Over Stress It Every Week.* It could become a ritual. People can become so used to hearing you stress a certain point that it becomes habit and they scarcely hear what you say; hence, do not stress it to the same extent each week. Stress it vehemently periodically, then just slightly between times.

9. *When You Know of Someone Who Is Ready to Be Saved, Give His Name to Someone Other than Yourself on Visitation Night.* When you know of someone who wants to be saved, and he is ready to be saved, and you feel sure that he can be won—send someone else to visit him rather than going yourself. This will give the one who goes a blessing and cement him into the visitation program of the church.

10. *After You Win Someone, Send Another by to See Him before Sunday.* After you have won someone to Christ yourself, as a leader in the church, why not go to one of your people whom you wish to encourage and give him the name of the person? Ask him to go by and visit the person whom you have won. Then, on Sunday when the person you won walks the aisle to make profession, it will be a blessing to the person who went to visit him, and encourage him to continue in the visitation program of the church. This may also prove successful with folks who have voiced their intentions of moving their membership. Send some of the members by to visit them. This will give them a feeling that they have had a part in reaching this family, and will give them a blessing.

11. *Have Different Persons Go Visiting with You.* As a leader in the church you can train soul winners by inviting people who are not soul winners to go with you in witnessing. As they see you win souls, they have themselves been instructed and taught how to win someone. The best soul winners we have in our church are people who have been with the pastor or some other soul winner and have personally seen the miracle happen.

12. *Opening Assembly Program.* One of the most effective ways to train soul winners is to show them. When you have won a soul during the week, have that person come with you to the opening assembly of Sunday school or the youth group and present a "skit" for the people. Show exactly what happened as you won the person, from start to finish. That will give your people firsthand information about how to win a soul.

13. *When a Member Wins a Soul Include This Fact in Your Sermon.* When you hear of one of your members winning a soul to Christ, give him just praise and reward in a public way by telling the people—either in announcing it, or including it in your sermon. Or, when the person comes down the aisle, let the soul winner come and stand beside the convert, and give due reward and credit to the soul winner.

14. *Do Not Wear the People Out.* There is such a thing as getting people tired in the service of the Lord. Certainly we should never tire of service for the Lord—but we can give our people so many things, including a number of nonessentials, that they can fail to be good witnesses for the Lord Jesus. If a church program is kept simple (teach the Bible, pray, visit) without too many "frills" on the side, then the people will not be so worn out they do not have time to visit.

15. *Give the People Some Nights to Stay at Home.* Many of our people are so busy doing other things that they feel they simply must have some nights at home, so they take the night at home which is usually given to visitation. It is my observation that if people know the pastor is trying to let them have some nights at home, then they will give the church more nights of service for Christ.

We have found it advisable to have two nights each week called "Stay at Home Nights," or "Lights Out at the Church Nights." Tuesday and Friday nights are good. We encourage our people not to go to any class meetings, parties or any other church gatherings on these two nights, except during revivals or Bible conferences.

3. How to Organize a Visitation Program

How should a visitation program be organized? What methods should be used? These and other questions are asked continually by church leaders, especially pastors. Some suggestions will be given in this chapter for use in organizing a visitation program.

1. *Have a Card File.* You may use a simple card file for your prospect cards. The NAME and ADDRESS of the prospect are all that you need on the card. Then, use the back of the card for writing a report on the results of your visit, and the date of the visit. This will keep the next visitor informed of the results of the previous visit. Any helpful information should be written on the back of the card for the visitor.

The pastor should go through the card file personally, and choose the people to be visited. As he goes through the file, he should pick out the ones whom he feels need visiting this particular week. The best prospects are those who have visited in the regular church services, the "new moves" into the city, and others who voice interest in coming.

It is good to separate the card file and set it up by town sections. This has been the most effective method for us. We have our city divided into twenty sections, and the cards are placed in their corresponding section. Below is a sample of one of our 4 x 6 prospect cards, which we mimeograph in our office.

There are many visitation card files you may use. All of them are good and may be found anywhere. However, the important thing in a visitation program is not the file—it is the way the file is used. This chapter is not to

(cut of one of our prospect cards)

PROSPECT CARD

NAME: John Doe   DATE: 11-20-57

ADDRESS: 123 Main Street

New Move to City: New Address: Other:

      (*check one*)

DATE OF VISIT: VISITED BY: RESULTS OF VISIT:

11-21-57 — Smith & Jones — Just moved in. Baptist.

Promised to visit us Sunday. Nice.

(*over*)

---

give you filing suggestions, or card suggestions, but to give you practical ways to use the files that have already been made.

2. *Do Not Have More Than Two Visitation Programs Each Week.* By having not more than two visitation programs each week, the efforts will be concentrated. Perhaps the wisest thing to do is to have the visitation program on one day — one session in the morning and one in the evening. The ladies may visit in the morning and the men at night, along with the ladies who work during the day.

3. *Do Not Have Too Many Other Activities in the Church Program.* Make visitation the biggest thing—make soul winning the most important thing in your church. Then the people will have time to do that which Jesus told us to do. Many churches are occupied with such varied activities that soul winning is pushed under the carpet. The visitation program should be the largest thing in the church. It should be better attended than softball games and other functions. Some churches have found it

best not to have the other activities, but major entirely on the soul winning and visitation itself.

4. *Thursday Is Often the Best Day for Visitation.* Our visitation program is on Thursday morning and Thursday night. The ladies come on Thursday morning (with some of the men who work at night) at ten o'clock; and the working ladies and men come at seven o'clock on Thursday night. Thursday is a good time for two reasons: First, it is close enough to Wednesday night so that no one forgets visitation. A reminder on Wednesday night is always in order. Second, it is near enough to Sunday that people who are visited can easily remember the promise they made. Monday is a good day to go visiting, but it is so far from the next Sunday that it is less effective than Thursday. However, I would suggest Monday as the second best for a visitation program. People forget easily. It is easier to get folks to come to the church on Monday or Thursday than any other time, because it is fresh on their minds after the services on Sunday and Wednesday.

5. *Have a Place for Everyone.* We have found it advisable to have something planned for each age group on visitation night. For example, in our church we have all of our nurseries open. We also have a planned period for the beginners and primaries. Workers from a different beginner or primary department are in charge of the beginner and primary children whose parents come to visit each week. This program includes singing, games (modeling clay, picture puzzles, etc.) conduct or child life stories, Bible stories (flannelgraph) and handwork of some kind. The handwork may be simple (color sheets or something to make from construction paper, etc.). Sometimes the children go outside for games and refreshments.

We also have a special program for our juniors on visitation night. They meet in the back yards of some of the workers' homes each week where they have a special time of fellowship and Bible study. This program for juniors may include special Bible memory work contests, and the children may be rewarded for their efforts.

We have our youth choir on Thursday night, which takes care of the young people. This leaves only the adults free to visit. A place is provided for everyone in the family. For a long time we noticed that a husband would come to visitation and his wife would stay home. Hence, we have practically doubled our efficiency by providing a place for each member of the family on Thursday morning and Thursday night.

6. *The Pastor Should Meet the People as They Come.* I have always tried to make it a practice before the services to stand outside and meet the people as they come —especially at visitation. If the people can meet the pastor, and chat for a while before they go visiting, it is a blessing. They feel that they have had God's man fellowshiping with them for a while.

7. *Compliment the people for Coming.* Many of us are hard on people who do not visit; it would be better to concentrate on being nice to those who do visit. A "God bless you," or a "I'm glad to see you tonight, John," or "It's a blessing to see you, Joe," means something to people. Also, a letter of thanks to those who have come for the first time will be appreciated by them, and will encourage them to participate regularly in the visitation program.

8. *Visit by Family Rather than by Age Group.* We have found it best to set-our files up by families rather than by age group. For example, if there are five people in a family and the visiting is done by the Sunday school classes, one family will get five visits—and four families will go unvisited. If we visit by families, not only does it mean that more families will be contacted, but it also means that people who work in the Sunday school with the younger children will have the opportunity to witness to adults. It also helps to keep the church one family, rather than several small churches within a church. We, therefore, have only one card for each family in our prospect files, rather than having one for each

member of the family, set up by Sunday school age groups.

9. *Have a Short Service Before You Go.* We find it helpful to have a song and a few testimonies—and just a short service before leaving to visit. Also, a period of prayer puts the people in a spiritual attitude before they go.

10. *Go Two by Two.* When the people arrive at the church, many of them have already chosen their visitation partners. Those who do not have partners should be carefully aided by the pastor in selecting visitation partners. People of mutual interests and social standing should be chosen to go together if at all possible.

11. *An Experienced and an Inexperienced Visitor Should Go Together.* Often the pastor should encourage the people to take inexperienced partners with them to visit. If two inexperienced people go together to visit, they might become discouraged and fail to return to visitation. However, if you can send an experienced visitor with each new person who comes, that will be an encouragement, as well as instruction to the new visitor.

12. *Give Only Five or Six Cards to Each Team Which Goes Visiting.* If a person can make two or three good visits a night he has done well. To do this, five or six cards would seem advisable. About fifty per cent of the people will not be at home; hence, the reason for giving several cards to each team.

13. *Place a Promising Prospect in Each Group of Cards.* If each group of cards has one good prospect in it, then each person who goes visiting will receive a blessing. As you group the cards, prior to visitation time, try to see that there is one good prospect in each group of cards, thereby assuring each visitor of at least one blessing. If they can come back from visiting feeling that they have done some good in at least one place, they will likely come back the next week.

14. *Leave In An Orderly Manner.* Be careful as you give the cards to the visitors. Some people can visit

better in certain sections of town than others. This selection may be done tactfully and carefully. Also, as the teams come by for their cards, give them doorknob hangers, literature about the church, tracts, and other items which can be used successfully in the visitation program.

15. *Have the Team Pray for Persons on Each Card.* One of the most successful things that we have ever done is to have a period of prayer by the team, after they are in their car, as they look at each card which has been given them. They call the name of the person on each card in prayer before they go.

16. *The Pastor Should Be Waiting for Them as They Return from Visiting.* Many people have won victories on visitation and they want to share them with the pastor. Many have had reversals they want to tell the pastor about. The pastor can rejoice with those who are rejoicing, and lament with those who are lamenting, encourage those who have not had good visits and thank them from the bottom of his heart for coming. This encourages the people, and gives them an opportunity to see the pastor before they leave to go home.

Another idea in getting folks to visit is to have folks who already come to visitation regularly solicit someone who does not come, previous to the visitation day, to go with them. If this could be done one particular week, the visitation crowd could be doubled in a week.

4. How to Win a Soul to Jesus

The purpose of this chapter is not to deal with witnessing in public, but it primarily concerns the winning of souls to Christ in the home. It deals with the proper approach and some practical pointers to help one be a more effective soul winner. I have tried to put these principles into practice for a number of years, and God has blessed them with the salvation of literally hundreds of souls being won to Him in homes. May God use them to bless you and make you a winner of souls for Christ.

Last year alone over three hundred of our people won someone to Christ. Each of them was instructed through the following method, which is simple and easy enough for anyone to understand.

1. *Be Clean and Neat.* If a person is going to be a soul winner he must not be offensive to the people with whom he talks. It is a definite asset for a soul winner to be careful to bathe often, to avoid body odor. Teeth should be brushed, and the breath should be tested. Carry mints in your pockets or some good flavored chewing gum which will help keep the breath from being offensive. One of the most damaging things in soul winning is the effect of halitosis. By all means, a soul winner should watch this carefully. The soul winner should also be neatly dressed. A lady should be dressed conservatively, and I think it is best for a man to at least wear a shirt with a tie.

2. *Carry a Testament with You All the Time.* One of the most effective methods that we have used is the carrying of *two* Testaments—one for you to read as you seek

to win the person, and one for the unsaved person to read, or follow as you read. After he has given his heart to Jesus, then you may present him with the Testament that he has read from as a gift.

Testaments which are adequate for. this type of work may be bought at most bookstores for about twenty-five cents each. It is our suggestion that a Testament is better to use than a Bible because it does not "give you away." As you get out of your car to walk to a house, a person might possibly see you carrying a Bible and immediately think that you are representing some cult or some false "ism" and build a mental barrier against you. Hence, it is usually better to carry a Testament in your pocket.

3. *Be Soul Conscious.* By this I simply mean to be aware everywhere you go that the people to whom you talk are going to spend eternity somewhere . . . the man who cuts your hair, the boy who shines your shoes, the man who fills your car with gas, the bread man, the milk man, the grocery man, the clerk at the drugstore, and the saleslady at the clothing store are *all* going to spend eternity somewhere. Make it a habit to ask people if they are Christians. This will be a blessing to you, and will give you a chance to witness to them. It is good to carry gospel tracts with you at all times in order that you may present one to a person who is not a Christian, that he may read it after you leave. This is effective to use when witnessing to people at work, who cannot stop their work for you to give them the plan of salvation.

Recently one of our soul winners was getting a shoe shine. Just before he asked the colored shine boy if he were a Christian, the shine boy looked up and asked the man if he were a Christian. Our church member responded with an affirmative answer, "Yes, you must be a Christian, too."

The colored boy replied, "Yes, sir, one of those Miller Road Baptist members won me to Jesus the other day while I was shining his shoes."

4. *Go Two by Two.* This is important! There are several reasons why God sent His disciples out in pairs,

and certainly we should follow His example. Also, there is strength in numbers, and with another Christian present as a prayer warrior the soul winner is encouraged. However, the most important reasons that another person should go with you, apart from Scriptural reason, are to pave the way for absolute quietness, and to avoid any unneccessary disturbances while the soul winner is talking to the unsaved person. Such things as caring for the children, changing the baby, answering the door, turning the radio or television off can certainly be of value in the winning of souls to Christ.

5. *Go with Different People.* Many people think it is wise to team up with the same soul winning partner all of the time. However, this discourages the making of new soul winners. It seems advisable for a person who is an active soul winner to take a different person with him periodically so that the new visitor might actually see the winning of a soul. This is better than any study course a Christian can take.

6. *Pray and Claim the Spirit Fullness before Going.* Before you go to the field you need to spend a few moments in prayer, simply asking God to bless you and to help you be a blessing to others. Also, claim His Spirit fullness by faith, asking Him to bless you as you go, and to prepare the hearts of those to whom you will talk.

7. *Go Believing.* The thing that transformed my soul winning life more than anything else was this one thing! Many times I would go to the fields to witness for Christ, not expecting to win anyone. When and if someone was converted I would actually be subconsciously surprised. However, it dawned on me one day that God wants to save people, and that as God was sending me out, He would save people. So, rather than going out defeated, an effort was made to go expecting to see someone saved. The increase that God gave to this attitude of faith was amazing.

8. *Be Nice.* Remember that the person to whom you are talking did not ask you to come. You are a guest in his home, and many times, an unwanted guest. A soul

winner in a home cannot use the same frankness that the preacher can in the pulpit. It is necessary that a soul winner be nice and courteous, kind and understanding, as he goes into someone's home to talk to him about the Lord.

9. *Be Careful about Going In.* If a person is busy and obviously does not want to be disturbed, many times it is wise to tell him that you will not come in at this particular time, and suggest that you make an appointment for a later date when you may come back and talk to him about the Lord. This has proven effective in many cases.

10. *Be Complimentary.* As you enter someone's home, it is always good to be complimentary. If the children are sweet, tell them so. If the home is lovely mention it. It is good to be complimentary.

11. *Let the One You are Visiting Talk of His Interests for a While.* Ask him about his work, about the family, about his home town, and things of that nature. He will enjoy talking with you and speaking of his interests. One of the best points that a person can use is to be a good listener.

12. *Have Only One Person Do the Talking.* As you seek to win the person to Christ, let only one soul winner do the talking. Do not interrupt with your "two cents." You keep the road clear and keep the way paved for their privacy and pray! Do not pray with your eyes closed, however, as you may miss a chance to be of help by giving a child a drink, answering the door, or other things which might cause the lost person not to be free to listen carefully to the soul winner.

13. *Stay on the Subject.* Many times as you try to win a person he will ask questions that are irrelevant to salvation. When such a question is asked, it is usually good to say, "That is a good question. Remind me in a moment and I will answer that." Then, continue talking about the plan of salvation. Do not let yourself be sidetracked on less important issues.

14. *Stay in the Same Book of the Bible.* It seems that

it would be confusing to a sinner for a soul winner to go all over the Bible in trying to explain his point. With isolated verses taken from all over the Scriptures anything can be proved; however, when a person stays in the same book of the Bible, near the same pages, the lost person can readily see that you are not trying to confuse him by taking isolated verses to prove your point. A good book to use is John, another one is Isaiah; however, I have found the most effective book to be Romans.

15. *Draw a Map in Your Testament.* Many people are young Christians and do not have the Scriptures memorized, nor can they find the ones that they must use to deal with the plan of salvation. To aid in this, a plan has been devised of drawing a map in the Bible or Testament one is using. For example, start with Romans 3:10. Then, beside Romans 3:10, write Romans 3:23, the next verse you will turn to. After you have explained Romans 3:23, have written beside this verse Romans 5:12, which shows you where to go from there. Then, Romans 6:23, Romans 5:8, and finally Romans 10:9-11.

The lost person will not necessarily see what you have written in your Bible, as he will be looking on from the other Testament which you have handed him to use. This way you can direct yourself to the next Scripture, even though you may not know a single Scripture by heart, or do not know where to find the Scriptures pertaining to the plan of salvation.

16. *Three Basic Questions Should Be Asked in the Conversation.* First ask, "Are you a Christian?" Second, "Would you like to be a Christian?" Third, "If I were to show you in the Bible how to be a Christian, would you be willing to do what God says?"

The first of these three questions has often been disputed. Some prefer to ask "Are you saved?", or, "Are you born again?", or, "Do you know Jesus?" However, the simple question, "Are you a Christian?" might lead to asking other questions. The way the person answers your question would determine whether or not you should inquire further as to the sincerity of his profession. Then, if he wants to be a Christian, you may proceed. Remember this—it is God's business to prepare a soul. You cannot argue anyone into being a Christian. He must be ready; if he is not ready, you cannot argue him into it. Then, if he commits himself by saying he would be saved if he knew how, you have a definite committal that he will respond. If he says he will, then proceed immediately to show him the aforementioned Scriptures.

Following is the structure of the conversation that I have found helpful in dealing with most unsaved people with whom I talk:

Soul winner: "First, Mr. Blank, if a person is going to be saved, he needs to be saved *from* something. Let me show you why a person needs to be saved. Notice in Romans 3:10, 'As it is written, There is none righteous, no, not one.' The word *righteous* means good; hence, there is none good, no, not one. If there is not *one* good—then I am not good. Is that right? If there is not one good, then you are not good. Is that right? Now, let us turn to Romans 3:23, 'For all have sinned, and come short of the glory of God.' If *all* have sinned, then that means that I have sinned. If *all* have sinned, that means you have sinned. So, you see that all of the people in the world are sinners. There is none that doeth good. We are all gone out of the way; we are together become unprofitable, and we have all sinned and come short of the glory of God.

"Now, Mr. Blank, may I show you where the sin came from? Notice in Romans 5:12, 'Wherefore, as by one man sin entered into the world, and death by sin; and so death passed upon all men, for that all have sinned.' You recall that one man brought sin into all the world. You will also remember that this man was Adam in the garden of Eden. God made Adam and Eve. He put them in the garden. He told them that they could eat of every tree in the garden but one, and if and when they ate of that tree, they would die. Do your remember, Mr. Blank, whether or not they ate of that tree?"

Mr. Blank: "Yes, they did."

Soul Winner: "Yes, they did. When they did, they were

separated from God. They died spiritually, and they became sinners. So, when they had children, their children were sinners, and *their* children were sinners, and *their* children were sinners—until finally, Mr. Blank, one day you were born, and the Bible says that you were born in sin. Though you were not accountable for it until you realized that you were a sinner, you were born going away from God. Mr. Blank, you are still going away from God; hence, you are a child of Adam.

"Now, would you look at and read Romans 6:23, 'For the wages of sin is death; but the gift of God is eternal life through Jesus Christ our Lord'?

"Mr. Blank, God, in order to be a just God, must make us pay for our sins. God has said that you will not get by with sin—so, God must make us pay for sin. The price on sin is death. This death is a spiritual death which culminates in the second death, mentioned in Revelation 21:8 and Revelation 20:14, which is the Lake of Fire. Therefore, the ultimate price that man must pay for his sins is to suffer in the Lake of Fire—or to go to hell. That means, Mr. Blank, according to your own statement that you are not a Christian, and according to the Word of God, if you died today you would go to hell. Is that right?"

Mr. Blank: "Yes."

Soul Winner: "Mr Blank, I am happy to tell you that God does not want you to go to hell. God loves you as you love your children. Just as you would make a way to save any wayward children of yours, even so God has made a plan to save you. Here is His plan. Please read Romans 5:8, 'But God commendeth his love toward us, in that while we were yet sinners, Christ died for us.' Mr. Blank, God looked down and saw that you were a sinner, and saw that you were going to hell. He did not want you to go to hell, so He came to earth in the form of a Man. His name was Jesus Christ. For thirty-three years He lived upon the earth—not once did He sin. Mr. Blank, if Jesus had sinned once, and the price of sin finally is the Lake of Fire, where would Jesus have had to go when He died?"

Mr. Blank: "To the Lake of Fire."

Soul Winner: "Exactly so. But He did not sin, did He?"

Mr. Blank: "No."

Soul Winner: "He was perfect. Not once did He have an evil thought, not once did He say a nasty word, not once did He drink a bottle of beer, not once did He do anything that was contrary to His Father's will. But Mr. Blank, on the Cross of Calvary Jesus Christ suffered spiritual separation from God, or the same thing that the sinner must suffer in hell. If He was not suffering it for His own sins, then He must have been suffering for someone else's sins. Do you have any idea for whom He was suffering?"

Mr. Blank: "He was suffering for you and me."

Soul Winner: "Exactly so. Now, if He was suffering for you and me, He was paying our debt. Is that right?"

Mr. Blank: "Yes."

Soul Winner: "Mr. Blank, if I went to the bank today, and paid off all of your debts at the bank, they would send a representative out to tell you about my payment. You would have one of two choices. You could say, 'No, I will not accept his payment; I will pay my own debts.' If that were your answer, even though I had paid the price, you would still be in debt. However, on the other hand, you could say, 'Of course, I will accept payment. I will receive the gift that Mr. Soul Winner gave me.' That moment, Mr. Blank, you would be free of debt. That moment the bank would wipe your debts completely clean. Now, Mr. Blank, you are in debt to God. You have sinned. Your record is in heaven. Jesus Christ went to the bank of heaven, as it were, and paid the full payment for all of your debts. He has paid for all of your sins. He sent me as His representative today to tell you about this. You can say one of two things: You can say, 'No, I will pay my own debts. I will go to hell for myself.' Or, you can say, 'Of course, I will accept a Saviour like that. I will accept His gift of eternal life, and receive

Him as my Saviour.' That moment, Mr. Blank, you become a child of God, by receiving Christ as a Substitute for your sin, and taking Him in your heart as your Saviour.

"Now, Mr. Blank, let us sum up what we have said. Do you realize that you are a sinner?"

Mr. Blank: "Yes."

Soul Winner: "Do you realize that if you died today you would go to hell?"

Mr. Blank: "Yes."

Soul Winner: "Do you realize that Jesus died in your place, and suffered spiritual separation from God in your place?"

Mr. Blank: "Yes."

Soul Winner: "Do you realize that if you were to bow here, and seek God's forgiveness and take Christ as your Saviour today, by faith, God would make you His child?"

Mr. Blank: "Yes."

Soul Winner: "Then, Mr. Blank, could we just bow our heads and hearts in prayer, and let me pray for you? While I pray you can consider giving your heart to the Lord Jesus. Shall we kneel?"

(Turn to Romans 10:13—read it to him and have him put his hand on that Scripture. You pray. Pray sincerely, simply and briefly. As you conclude your prayer, do not say "Amen.")

Soul Winner: "With our heads bowed, Mr. Blank, wouldn't you like to ask God to forgive your sins right now? Tell Him that you are sorry for your sins, tell Him you want to receive Christ as your Saviour now. Will you do it?" (Mr. Blank may pray a simple prayer. If not, you might ask him to pray after you sincerely.)

Soul Winner: "Mr. Blank, if you are willing now, the best you know how, to turn from sin, and give your heart to Christ in faith, would you please take my hand as if it were the hand of Jesus as a token thereof?" (Mr. Blank takes the soul winner's hand. The soul winner, while holding the convert's hand, should offer a prayer of thanksgiving to God for saving him.)

Soul Winner: "God bless you, Mr. Blank. Now, let me ask you a question. If the Bible is true—where would you go if you died now?"

Mr. Blank: "I would go to heaven."

Soul Winner: "Isn't that wonderful? Isn't God good to give eternal life to those who will receive him by faith?"

17. *Lead Him to a Profession.* After the person has been converted, ask him to promise to come to church the next possible service, and walk the aisle and let the pastor tell the people that he has been saved. It seems unwise to ask him to be baptized until he has made his profession. Then, at the altar, when he is making his profession, or later, the minister can speak with him about baptism.

18. *Go by and Get the Convert the Next Sunday.* It is an unusual experience for many new converts to come to church. Many of them have not been to church for months, or years. It would be much easier for them to come if you will offer to go by and bring them with you.

19. *Sit with the Convert in the Service.*

20. *At the Close of the Service Offer to Go Down the Aisle with Him.*

21. *After He Has Made His Profession, United with the Church and Been Baptized, He is Still Your Child.* Continue to watch over him, and help him. Ask him over to your house for refreshments. Fellowship with him, and make him feel at home in the service of the Lord.

22. *Appoint a Committee to Go by and See the New Converts, as Well as the New Church Members.* The week after they join the church, it is good to have a committee to go by and see the new converts and new members. This group may carry a certificate of baptism, a copy of the church budget, a copy of some book advising young Christians how to grow in grace, any books written by the pastor, etc. These will be helpful and appreciated by the new converts and new church members.

23. *Use the "Buddy" System.* After the Sunday services each week, call someone who lives near the new convert and "assign" him the new convert. It is good for him

to have the new convert over for refreshments, to make a visit into his home, and perhaps have his family over for a meal to try to get him acquainted with some of the church members.

This person's job also would be to help integrate the convert into the church program, and introduce him to as many people as possible.

5. Our New Visitation Program

By JIM LYONS, *Associate Pastor*

Our church has been fortunate in that the city in which we are located has, for a number of years, been one of the fastest growing cities in the State of Texas. Hundreds of prospects were moving into the city every month. This meant that our pastor could encourage all of the members to come out to our visitation program, and be able to supply each of them with some prospects to visit.

However, in the past year our city has ceased its rapid growth, and now only a few people move into our city each month. This meant, of course, that we would either have to find some other place to secure prospects—or else not encourage all of our people to come to the visitation program. We did not wish to choose the latter, as visitation is one of the biggest blessings that the church membership can have.

So the eight following means of visitation are carried out each Thursday night by the Miller Road Baptist Church in our new visitation plan.

1. *The Jails.* Two of our finest Christian men do no form of visiting on Thursday nights other than jail visitation. Our city jail will usually have at least a couple of people in it each week, and sometimes has as many as ten or twelve. We feel that when Jesus died for everyone, certainly we should overlook no one in our visitation program. These two men have been highly successful in their jail visitation, and have seen numbers of people saved since the institution of our new visitation

program, which included visiting the jails each week.

2. *The Hospitals.* Each week two or three teams composed of husbands and wives go to local and Dallas hospitals to visit those of our membership who are in the hospitals, and others who have been reported to the church office. They go for two purposes: First, to have prayer with those who are sick and ask God to heal their bodies. Second, they go to witness to those others who are in the rooms with the hospital patients from our church. Just recently one of our men went to see a person from our church who was in the hospital, and while visiting with the patient next to him, was able to win an eighty-year-old man to the Lord.

3. *Tract Distribution in Shopping Centers.* Each week we have three teams of four men each which distribute gospel tracts in shopping centers all over Dallas County. These men also go every time there is a great gathering of people for some special occasion—for instance, at the time our state fair was in progress, these men went each Thursday night and distributed thousands of tracts to people who were attending the fair. Hardly a week goes by that we do not receive a tract back through the mail, signed by someone saying that he has accepted Christ as his Saviour. Recently several of our fellows were passing out tracts in a shopping center that was just being opened. Many gifts were being given away on the formal opening night. The people at the shopping center, naturally thinking of the gifts that were being given out, formed a line to receive gospel tracts. Soon a long line had formed, and people were waiting to receive a gospel tract. You can imagine the surprised look on their faces when they got to the person who was handing out the tracts and found that they had stood in line to receive the Gospel.

4. *Beer Joints.* Our church is primarily a men's church. We have probably as large a percentage of men in our church as any church in the world. Many of these fellows only a few years ago, were drunkards far down in sin. Beer joints are nothing new to these men, and several

of them go each week to pass out tracts and witness to those in the beer joints, honky tonks and night clubs around Dallas County. This group is headed by a man who, by his own testimony, in a period of ten years did not see over ten days during which he failed to take a drink of liquor. This man was saved a few years ago, and now spends much of his time witnessing to the same crowd he once drank with. Hardly a week passes that this group does not bring one or several people to our church services on Sunday whom they have won on visitation night.

5. *Bus Stations.* One group of our men makes a regular Thursday night itinerary, which includes several of the bus stations and train terminals in Dallas. Many a person has found Jesus on Thursday night while sitting in a terminal waiting for his bus or train. Recently a young man seventeen years of age who had run away from his home in Kentucky, was found at the bus terminal. This young man gave his heart to Christ, came to the church and was baptized, has now found a job and is making his home in Garland. He is faithful to all services of the church.

6. *Absentee Visitation.* When a church reaches the size that our church has, there are many, many absentees each Sunday. We have found that the best way to visit these is in the church-wide visitation program on Thursday night. Each week someone from each class takes the "Absentee Book" and visits those who were not in Sunday school the previous Sunday from that particular class. This, of course, brings our people in contact with the entire family, giving them an opportunity to witness to those in the family who are not saved.

7. *House to House Visitation.* The last group to leave on Thursday nights from our chapel where we assemble for visitation, is the group which goes to visit in the homes in Garland. Even after sending someone to the jails, the hospitals, the shopping centers, the beer joints, the bus stations and to visit absentees, we still have quite a number of people left to visit from house to house

in Garland. This group visits in pairs. They go to visit those who have just moved into our city, those who have visited in our church services, or those whose names have been turned in to the office as possible prospects for the church, or persons who need to be witnessed to. Many, many people have been won to Christ in our house to house visitation by the members of our church. On a recent Sunday morning a couple came down the aisle and united with our church. In talking to them, we found that the man had been won to Christ by two of our men while visiting from house to house in our city. After talking a little further, we found also that at a different time, one of our ladies had gone by and had won the wife to Christ. What a blessing it is to see people come to Christ, regardless of where they are found.

8. *Visiting New Members.* Our last type of visitation on Thursday nights is the visiting of those people who have come into the fellowship of our church. One of our deacons, accompanied by his wife, goes and visits each person who joins our church. We have found this to be an effective means of visitation, in that others in the family who are lost or unchurched are contacted in this way. Recently while visiting a new member of our church, our deacon found that a couple was visiting from out of the city. Before long, this couple had given their hearts to Christ there in the home.

Our church, in the period of time since it has been organized, has received many, many blessings, but perhaps the greatest blessings that we have received have been trying to carry out the Great Commission in the vicinity in which we live.

6. A Realistic Approach to an Evangelistic Preaching Service

One of the most important things that the preacher does is preach. Of utmost importance in the life of the church is the public worship service. It is the time when the Gospel is preached and sinners are invited to the Lord Jesus Christ. The public service is the important thing in the life of a church!

Following are a number of rules which might be helpful in conducting an evangelistic worship service:

1. *The Pastor Should Be There.* It is important that the pastor be in his own pulpit. I have made it a policy through the years to be in my own pulpit every Sunday. Some preachers would not feel this advisable, and certainly that is understandable. However, as much as possible, the pastor should be in his own pulpit.

2. *Claim the Spirit Fullness.* If a preacher is prayed up as he should be, and talks to the Lord periodically, he should be able to preach all the time. Simply a prayer of claiming the Spirit fullness before he goes into the pulpit, is sufficient many times. Many preachers ruin their disposition, their sermon and their spirit by waiting too late on Saturday night to agonize, or, by waiting too late on Sunday morning. The agonizing should be done previous to the service, and a simple claiming by faith the fullness of God's spirit will many times suffice before the service. This does not discount the agonizing in prayer and the many hours a preacher should pray for the services and for the power of God—but the preacher should realize that God wants to fill him, and if he has met the conditions of God all week long in his life, then he can have His fullness on Sunday.

3. *Have Real Humility.* Humility is not cowardice; neither is it timidity. Humility is a feeling that "I can do all things through Christ which strengtheneth me." There is a fine line of distinction between a person who is "cocky," and a person who is humble. A cocky person says, "I can do all things." A humble person says, "I can do all things . . . through Christ."

4. *Work on Yourself before the Service.* Before the service, go alone and ask God to put you in the mood of the sermon. If you are going to preach against sin, think how awful sin is—ask God to stir your heart against it, and make you realize how dirty and black it is. If you are going to preach on heaven, try to walk the golden streets a while before you go into the pulpit. If you are going to preach on hell, turn the lights out for a while and think about how awful hell must be, and ask God to put you in the right mood for the sermon. This is important!

5. *Get Everyone to Participate in the Preaching Service.* That is one reason for the song service. If the people sing, and participate in the first part of the service, they will be relaxed for the invitation. Many churches find it wise to have the people shake hands at the first part of the service. This may become a formality if not handled properly. The people should definitely be loosened up in the early part of the service, and feel themselves a part of it. Many people never feel like part of the service, but like spectators. This should not be.

There are several ways the right feeling can be achieved. As mentioned before, hand-shaking is a good way. Then, a definite effort to get *all* of the congregation to sing in the song service is good. To do this, some old songs must be used, which all of the people will know.

Also, it is good to have a time to recognize visitors—to have them stand, say a few words about them, make them feel at home.

6. *Get concerned People to Lift Their Hands.* Sometimes in the early part of the service, it is often good to have the people bow their heads for prayer. Then ask

the people who are praying for an unsaved friend in the service to lift their hands. This will do several things: First, it will let you know if you have many prospects. Again, it will let you know the people in your church who bring lost souls to the services. Also, the person who raises his hand indicating that he is interested in a lost one, will usually be sitting next to or near the unsaved friend. This will let you know who the unsaved are so that you will be able to give them special attention later in the service.

7. *Preach to Get Results.* Preach to get results! Never become the teacher type or the lecturer type, and never get used to a "dry haul." When you preach a sermon on tithing, expect people to start tithing. When you preach against a certain sin, expect people to give it up. Always expect additions and conversions in the services. Preach to get results!

8. *Train the People to Be Openly for You.* This should be especially true when the preacher is a frank person. The visitors in the service, especially the unsaved, need to be conscious of the fact that the people there are for you, and believe what you are preaching. If they feel as if you are fighting an uphill battle and that the people are against what you say, your sermon will be ineffective. However, if they feel that in the power of the Spirit you are preaching Jesus in such a way that your people are for you, then they, too, will be impressed with the service.

Train your people to say "Amen" often. It is certainly helpful in an evangelistic preaching service.

9. *Do Not Reveal the Closing Point.* Many of us in our preaching will make such statements as, "Now, in conclusion"; "Finally, may I say"; "My last point is . . . ." These statements are sometimes dangerous. The sinner knows five minutes before you finish; hence, he digs in and prepares himself for the invitation so that he does not respond. However, if your closing is abrupt and a lost person does not suspect that you are about finished, you have crept up on him and he will not have time to

prepare himself for the invitation. Many people may be reached, using this method.

One of the most glaring errors of many churches is that just as the preacher nears the conclusion in his sermon, the organist tiptoes like a sniper in battle, to the organ, letting the people in the congregation know that invitation time is near—and letting the lost person brace himself for the invitation. Then the choir director whispers the number to the choir, and they begin to shuffle pages. We eliminate that in our church by using the same invitation hymn at the close of each service. If there is a change, the pastor announces the number at the beginning of the service. The invitation should be abrupt—the people should not have their attention diverted until time for the invitation itself.

10. *Do Not Fuss over Past Sins.* Many preachers ruin their effectiveness by preaching against the sins the members committed during the past week. They cannot undo a single one of them. However, they would do well to preach against the sins they might commit next week, and lead them to avoid those.

11. *Do Not Close the Service on a Low Note.* It is good to start the service on a high spiritual plane and to close the service on a high spiritual plane. If there is any skinning, or roof-raising to be done, do it in the middle of the sermon. Then, bring the sermon back up to a high spiritual level. People have a way of remembering the last part of the service. If the service is closed on a complaining, fussing note, then the people subconsciously register that and are not as prone to return. However, if the service is closed on a high note, a victorious note, all the time, then the people will subconsciously have the desire to come back.

12. *Do Not Ask for Rededications Until Souls Have Been Reaped.* Reap the souls first. Many times preachers have people come to kneel at the altar to rededicate their lives, begin family altars or begin tithing, and clog the aisles so that the lost people cannot get down them. Always try to reap the sinners first. Then, afterwards turn

to the Christians and lead them to a deeper life. Do not block the aisles with Christians so that the lost will be discouraged from coming.

13. *Use Soul Winners in the Invitation.* This is dangerous sometimes; however, it can be used effectively.

Have some key people in your church (many times some deacons) observe as the hands are raised for prayer in the invitation. Then, after singing a while, if these who raised their hands do not come, they may be approached by the soul winners, who may be able to lead them to Christ.

Promiscuous wandering around during the invitation is often hurtful. It should be guarded carefully in order not to hurt people, and lead folks farther away from Christ. However, when a person raises his hand, he is under conviction, and usually can be won by an effective, tactful, Spirit-filled soul winner.

It is hoped that the foregoing suggestions will be helpful to many pastors as they lead their churches to be evangelistic centers. God knows that if we worship in Spirit and in truth we will bring sinners to Christ week by week.

For the past forty-two months in the Miller Road Baptist Church someone has been saved every week, and someone has been ready for baptism each Sunday evening. May God be praised! These methods have been used of the Lord week after week in the bringing of souls to Christ. May God use them to bless your heart.

7. Big Days and Special Occasions

Big days are important in the lives of all Americans. Whether we like to admit it or not, we make much of big days and special occasions. Few are the families who do not get together during the Christmas season. Many thousands of us observe with joy the Thanksgiving season; Labor Day weekend also means much to Americans. We look forward with anticipation to big days, special occasions, long weekends and the holiday seasons. If this is so effective commercially and politically, then certainly it could be useful when carried into the life of a church. Many churches have found it advisable to use big days and special occasions with which to keep their people happy and aggressive, and to build their attendance. These days have been used effectively in places where I have been in Bible conferences and revivals. One church went from an attendance of 289 one Sunday to 1,080 the following Sunday! Many pastors and churches will testify to the help gained from the use of these and other suggestions for big days and special occasions.

This chapter is devoted largely to describing a number of the big days that we found helpful in our church program. Certainly no one person will agree with all of these occasions; and yet, if perchance a few might gain an idea or suggestion which will help their church work and increase their attendance, thereby bringing more souls to Christ, we will be grateful to the Lord Jesus.

OLD-FASHIONED DAY

Old-Fashioned Day is one of the most joyous days in our church. We do not set a specific attendance goal on this day, but we do try to have it on a weekend that would normally have a lower attendance than usual. For example, a good time for Old-Fashioned Day is the Fourth of July weekend, or the Labor Day weekend. We usually send out some sort of a mimeographed letter inviting our folk to the services on this day.

This day is filled with wonderful events which always bring a great deal of joy to our people. Let us note some of the things that we do on Old-Fashioned Day:

1. *Collection of Antiques.* After Old-Fashioned Day has been announced, and we begin to publicize it, we ask our people to bring antique items for display on the platform. Such items as old-fashioned churns, wash pots, spinning wheels, clocks, Bibles, curling irons and smoothing irons are brought and displayed for this special day. Many, many people have old-fashioned items which they like to bring and display. Then, on Old-Fashioned Sunday, these items are taken one by one and shown and explained to the congregation. It is always a source of joy and enthusiasm when these items are shown and memories are recalled.

Especially is this good for the older people. In many of our churches the program is geared for the younger people so much that the older people are forgotten. On an occasion like this, it gives the older members of the church a real opportunity to participate, to be blessed and to have a good time in the Lord Jesus.

2. *Pump Organ.* In order to help us have the old-fashioned spirit on this day, we have an old-fashioned pump organ on the platform. The organist usually plays a solo on the pump organ. Also, the offertory is played on the pump organ, which lends an old-fashioned atmosphere to the service.

It is a good idea to have two organists available to play the organ. After "pumping" for a while, a member of this modern generation will tire of pumping an organ. So, it is good to have a "spare" in case fatigue overtakes the first organist. This also gives the people a little levity, which helps the service.

3. *Hats Passed Instead of Plates.* Someone is appointed in advance to be chairman of the "Hat Committee," and he secures enough hats to pass to take the offering on this day.

4. *Mourner's Bench.* Someone is appointed to be in charge of a "Mourner's Bench." Any kind of old bench may be used, with some old quilts thrown over it. The Mourner's Bench across the altar lends much to the old-fashioned atmosphere on Old-Fashioned Day. Remember, many people were converted at the old-fashioned Mourner's Bench, under a brush arbor or in a tent campaign. It will recall many memories to have the Mourner's Bench. In fact, every church should provide some kneeling place at the altar where sinners may come and confess their sins and talk to God in the altar of the church.

5. *Creek Baptizing.* When promoting Old-Fashioned Day make much of the Creek Baptizing. The church members assemble about 3:30 in the afternoon and form a processional of cars to a near-by creek, and the converts for that week are baptized in the creek. Pictures of the creek baptizing are always taken.

Sometimes it is good to secure a Model T Ford to lead the processional. A good time is in store for everyone, as well as a spiritual blessing in the old-fashioned creek baptizing.

6. *Coal Oil Lamps and Lanterns.* On Old-Fashioned Day the only lighting that is used is coal oil lamps and lanterns. About three weeks in advance of this special day, the pastor may appoint a committee to assemble enough lamps and lanterns to light the auditorium fairly well. These may be lit for the morning service; and then they also provide all of the necessary light for the evening service. The evening service on Old-Fashioned Day is truly a blessing, as the people come and worship God, sing and hear the Word of God preached in an old-fashioned atmosphere with coal oil lamps and lanterns.

7. *Old-Fashioned Costumes.* Some may want to wear old-fashioned costumes, or maybe overalls for the men, on this day. However, in our own particular situation,

it is unadvisable. We do, however, for the opening assembly of the Sunday school, have all of the adults assemble for a skit, using old-fashioned gay nineties costumes. The preacher wears a tall black hat, with cutaway coat. Other leaders in the church wear similar costumes. This is good only for an opening assembly and not for the regular service, as it would detract from the purpose of the service. This is a joyous occasion.

Costumes for this occasion may be secured from any costume shop and are certainly in keeping with the occasion. These costumes may also be worn in the Model T Ford on the way to the baptismal service in the afternoon.

8. *Other Suggestions.* Keep in mind during Old-Fashioned Day and other special occasions the idea of taking pictures. Numbers of the people will want to bring their cameras, some will bring movie cameras and can preserve the spirit of the day for future years. These pictures will certainly be a blessing as the years go by.

It is good for the song leader to select old-fashioned songs, for the pastor to preach a sermon on the old time religion and have some old-fashioned testimonies. This is especially good in the night service when the coal oil lamps and lanterns furnish the only light.

Old-Fashioned Day is one of the highlights of our church year. A number of people are converted on this day each year. God has been good to us on this wonderful day. There is not a day in the year when our people are happier in the Lord than they are on Old-Fashioned Day.

Of course, one must remember to keep Jesus in the center of it all, remember that He is an old-fashioned Saviour, with an old-fashioned Gospel, that will take people to an old-fashioned heaven and save them from an old-fashioned hell, by the way of the old-fashioned Cross, written about in the old-fashioned Book empowered by the old-fashioned Spirit of God.

Below is a sample of one of the letters which we mail to each member of our church and Sunday school the week preceding Old-Fashioned Day.

OLD-FASHIONED DAY
SUNDAY, JULY 14TH

Telephone, visit, or write your FRIENDS, RELATIVES and NEIGHBORS and invite them to be with us for Old-Fashioned Day, THIS SUNDAY!!

Be sure to come in time for Sunday school at 9:30 a.m.! In the Adult Assembly there will be a SPECIAL program, with the deacons in their overalls, the pastor and Brother Bill in old-fashioned suits, a display of old-fashioned items on the platform—good old-fashioned singing, and many other interesting things in store for you at SUNDAY SCHOOL!

Plan to Attend Every Service This Sunday!!

Below is a wonderful piece of poetry (?) written by the pastor, which will tell you more about OLD-FASHIONED DAY.

A BREEF AND KORECK PEECE OF POITRI

Bi Edger Alin Po

I ain't much uv a poet, you kno,
I hav the hardes' tyme
Makin' the lions come out jist rite
An makin' the virses rime,

But Ole-fashuned Day iz hear again.
THIS SUNDAY iz the day
Whin we ditch this modernn stuph
And do the ole tyme way.

We're goin' to hav a mournir's binch
Wher folks kan kneel and pray
And git our kold harts rite with God
Just lyke the old time way.

Wee shud be verry dignafide
So miny peeple say,
But I'd ruther sing and shout "amen"
Az they did en yistarday.

We're goin' to hav an old pump orgin
For Mrs. Lions to pla
We're goin' to sing the old time songs
And preech the old time way.

I'm goin' to babtiz en the creak
Just like John the Baptist did.
Miny use a baptistri;
We're goin' to uze the creke instid.

We're goin' to burn cole oil lamps
And laturns on that day
Won't it be funn to wurshipp God
En the ole-fashuned way?

Bily Rosenbum iz goin' to sing
With the quartett duin' itz part.
They're goin' to sing that ole song
"I've gott that old tyme relijun in mi hart."

Yes, ther iz goin' two be lotz of funn
Down on Miller Rode
So kome to Sunday skul and church
And brink a hole kar lode.

The Church's Birthday

Secure the birthday or anniversary of the church, and once each year celebrate the church's birthday. We have this big day in our church in March each year. Some of the things that we consider important on this day are as follows:

1. *A Birthday Cake.* Our birthday cake is usually a huge one. The most recent one that we had weighed over five hundred pounds and was quite expensive; however, smaller cakes may be used effectively.

One thing to note in making the cake is that you may make the cake appear to be much larger than it is by building a form and putting cake around it. Much of it may be wood with icing over it, which makes it look larger.

We have made it a practice each year to raise money to pay for the cake apart from the church budget. It has long been our conviction that the money given in tithes and offerings should be used for spreading the Gospel; hence, there are ways, such as special offerings, whereby money for the birthday cake may be raised. This is advisable in many churches where this idea has been used.

Another idea for the cake is that it may be designed in various shapes. One year ours was a cross and a Bible. The most recent and the largest cake that we have used was a replica of our church buildings. This was the most popular cake that we have ever used.

2. *The Candles.* One way we promote attendance on our birthday is by mailing a letter to each person enrolled in our Sunday school the week preceding the birthday. A small birthday candle is enclosed in each letter. Each member is asked to bring his candle to Sunday school on Sunday morning. The candles may be collected during Sunday school and turned in with the records. Then, they are all placed on the cake at the same time. Be sure that *each* child is mailed a candle. It gives an incentive to come to the birthday party, when they will have their own candles placed on the cake.

Many times attendance goals are set for each class or department. We have large candles available for each teacher or department who reaches the goal. At the close of the Sunday school hour, after everyone is assembled in the auditorium, just before the morning service, the teachers or superintendents who reached their goals are recognized. They light their large candles and place them on the cake. The candles are blown out by the deacons, as the congregation sings "Happy Birthday."

3. *In the Afternoon.* On our "Birthday Sunday" the church meets outside someplace in the afternoon, or perhaps in a community house, to eat the cake. The drinks are usually provided by some of the members or by a special offering.

It is a good time of fellowship as the members get together and eat cake, with some soft drinks. Usually we have so much cake because of the size that ours have been, that many members take home a pound or so with them.

4. *Special Guests.* On the church's birthday celebration it is always good to invite people who are acquainted

with the founding of the church and the early days of the church's history, to come in to give testimonies about the church. Converts may also be recognized, as well as charter members.

This is not only a good day for remembering the history of the church, but also to make vows for the future.

5. *Birthday Party Letter*:

Please Come to the Big Birthday Party of the
Miller Road Baptist Church
This Sunday, March 13th,
9:45 A.M.

You will have "loads of fun" if you will do the following:

1. Bring the enclosed CANDLE with you to Sunday school so we can put it on our *huge* 200 pound cake!

2. Be here, by all means, at 9:45 to help us reach our attendance goal of ". . . 1003 on the day we're 3 . . . ."

3. Be at the Community House at 5:00 p.m. where we will serve our cake.

4. Be in training union at 6:30 p.m. to hear Dr. Fred Schwarz, a noted authority on Communism.

5. BY ALL MEANS, be here in time for Sunday school . . .

SPECIAL RECOGNITION will be given in the preaching service to each class or department reaching their goal!!

See you at the party . . .

S U N D AY , 9:45!

BACK TO SCHOOL DAY

Another day which we make much of at our church is Back to School Day. This day is celebrated on the first or second Sunday after school has started each fall. Following are some of the ideas that we use for this day:

1. *Personal Letters to School Students*. The pastor writes a personal letter to all of the school students— one to each child, whether in the first grade or a senior in high school. In this letter he reminds them of Back to School Day in their honor the following Sunday, and invites them to come. He also reminds them of the special gift to be given to each pupil who comes. Of course, this

special day has been publicized from the pulpit several times previous to the time that the letters are sent out.

This letter may be mimeographed; however, it is a good idea to leave the salutation blank so that each child's name may be written in longhand—for example, "Dear Sally," or "Dear John." Also, if possible, it is a good idea *not* to mimeograph the signature, but rather for the pastor to *sign* each letter personally. This makes the child feel that it is a *personal* letter, especially to him. Children, especially the smaller ones, have not yet heard about mimeograph machines. It will be like getting a personal letter from their pastor. Many children have been thrilled over receiving such correspondence, and you might be surprised at the increase it makes in the Sunday school attendance. Below is a sample letter:

M I L L E R   R O A D   B A P T I S T   C H U R C H
G A R L A N D ,   T E X A S
    from the
OFFICE OF THE PASTOR   September 10, 1956

.... ,

Did you start back to school last week?? If you did, this is a "personal" letter from ME to YOU! I want to tell you about the BIG DAY that we are having in your honor at Sunday school and church THIS Sunday morning, September 16th!!

First, let me congratulate you on the step you have taken in starting the school year. Next, let me invite you to be SURE and be in Sunday school next Sunday morning at 9:30! Here are the reasons that I ESPECIALLY want YOU to come:

(1) I have a nice gift to give you. Every school student who attends Sunday school this Sunday will receive a nice gift. It will be something that you will want to keep—something that you can take to school with you every day—something that we have never given away on back-to-school day before. It is a nice ball point pen *with the name of your church* and *a verse of Scripture printed*

on it!! It will be a *beautiful* pen that you will enjoy using and will want to keep always!

THE ONLY WAY THAT YOU CAN GET ONE IS TO BE IN SUNDAY SCHOOL THIS SUNDAY MORNING AT 9:30!! It will be a daily witness for Jesus in school!

(2) We will recognize you in the preaching service. We want you to stand up so that the entire congregation can see you!

(3) I will be preaching a special sermon in your honor, and I want you to hear it.

DON'T FORGET NOW . . . THIS SUNDAY, SEPTEMBER 16th, at 9:30 a.m.!! Hope to see YOU then.

I hope that you will have a good school year, that you will study hard and make good grades, and be a real Christian young person for Jesus.

Sincerely your pastor,

2. *The Gifts.* On Back to School Day each school child receives a special gift during the Sunday school hour. There are a number of gift items which may be used. One year we presented the students with little combs with a verse of Scripture on them, along with rulers. Another year we gave pencils with a Scripture on them. In more recent years we have given nicer gifts. For example, one year we gave tablets with the church's name at the top of each sheet, with a Scripture verse and "Jesus Saves" at the bottom of each page. Still another year we gave each child a ball point pen, with the name of the church, the pastor and a verse of Scripture on each pen. This is one good way to help the students in their witnessing at school.

3. *Special Reserved Section.* It is sometimes good to reserve a special section in the auditorium for the school children, if there is room for such. This makes them feel more honored. At any rate, they should be given special recognition in the church service.

4. *Using the Students in the Service.* It is good if you can use school students to take the offering, act as ushers, sing the special music, give a testimony and other things in the service which seem advisable.

5. *Inviting the School Teachers.* Something that we have not used heretofore, but which we plan to use next year, is the idea of having a special reserved section for all of the school teachers of the children. Insist for several weeks ahead that each child solicit the attendance of his school teacher on Back to School Sunday. Of course, this will necessitate having the day several weeks after school starts, perhaps near the first of October. Many teachers would be blessed and honored by such a service. Perhaps, also, the Gospel might be preached to some who otherwise would not hear it. If the teachers could feel the spirit of a warm, spiritual service, it would perhaps open their minds toward many churches which may be considered a little "narrow-minded" because of convictions. At least it would help the relationship between the school and the church.

6. *The Sermon.* The preacher may adapt his sermon to the school students, preaching such subjects as "Back to School with Jesus," "How to Live for Christ at School," or some other appropriate subject for the day.

Many school students may be reached for Christ through a special day like Back to School Day who would not otherwise come to Sunday school and the morning service.

Baby Day

Every church would do well to have Baby Day. This is a big day in our church and we usually have it in the spring. Many parents have babies who were born during the winter months and who have never been to church. The parents may be out of the habit of coming, and a special day in honor of the babies will get them back to God's house. Also, it serves as a time of dedication for the precious babies that God has given us during the past year.

If your church is small, you may recognize and honor *all* of the children, three years of age and under. In large churches, however, only the small babies can be recognized —those who have not reached their first birthday.

1. *Special Letter.* For this occasion you may send out

a special letter to the baby. Address it to the baby, telling him that you have a corsage for his mother, and that you are having a *special* day for him. Explain to him that you are happy that he is here. Who knows but what it will be the first letter ever addressed to the new baby.

This is the letter we sent:
Dear Parents,

Each year in our church we set aside one Sunday to honor all of the children in the nursery departments of our Sunday school. This Sunday, May 5th, is the day for this special occasion—BABY DAY!!

We know that you will want to have your child present for this special day in their honor. Here's what we will do:

Immediately at the close of the Sunday school hour, bring your child from the Nursery Department into the AUDITORIUM. BEFORE the preaching service, there will be a PARADE of all the nursery children around the auditorium and across the platform. All babies who have not reached their first birthday will be introduced from behind the pulpit!!!

Little pink corsages will be presented to all mothers of little girls; little blue corsages to all mothers of little boys!!!

This is one of the sweetest days in our church year. DON'T MISS IT!!! This gives all of our people an opportunity to see and meet your baby. Many of us who do not have occasion to go to the nursery department miss the blessing of seeing the nursery children.

ALSO, it gives the people a chance to meet the nursery workers who faithfully care for the children each Sunday while we worship.

So, be SURE to have your child here THIS SUNDAY morning at 9:30 a.m. for Sunday school, and for the BABY PARADE immediately following Sunday school!!!

There will be a *special place reserved* in the auditorium for the parents of the nursery children to sit during the preaching service!!!

We are counting on YOU to help us make this the
BIGGEST and BEST "BABY DAY" we have ever had!!!
Sincerely,
Your Pastor

2. *The Nursery Workers.* At the morning service special
recognition is given to those who work with the babies all
of the time. The nursery teachers in the Sunday school,
as well as the paid nursery workers, should be recognized. Each worker is presented with a lovely corsage, as
she is introduced to the congregation by the pastor.

3. *Baby Parade.* At the conclusion of the Sunday school
hour, each parent goes to the nursery and gets his child,
and brings him to the auditorium. The parents, with their
babies, are lined up around the auditorium. After the
nursery workers have been introduced and presented with
their corsages, the pianist or organist plays "Jesus Loves
Me" or some other appropriate song, as the parents "parade" their babies around the auditorium. Each parent
comes behind the microphone on the platform, shows the
congregation the baby, and tells his or her name.

4. *Corsages.* You may present small corsages to each
mother of a new baby—that is, mothers of babies born
since last Baby Day, or who are less than one year old.
Mothers of little boys may be presented with *blue* corsages, mothers of little girls with *pink* corsages. These
may be bought inexpensively, and may be made of just
one carnation and some ribbon.

These corsages may be presented to the mothers during
the Baby Parade as they come behind the pulpit to introduce their babies. The paid nursery workers may assist
the pastor or Sunday school superintendent in presenting the corsages, thereby saving some time.

5. *Altar Dedication Service.* After corsages have been
presented to the workers and to the mothers, and the
babies have been "paraded"—just before they are re-
turned to the nurseries—each parent may bring his baby
to the altar and the pastor may have a special prayer
of dedication, for God to bless the life of each baby, that

Jesus might have His will in their lives and in the lives of the parents.

It is also fitting to have a special musical number while the parents are at the altar, with heads bowed. There are many special numbers about children, or perhaps the music director might write one suitable for the occasion. The song may be sung first, after which the pastor may lead in the prayer of dedication.

6. *Reserve Section for Parents.* After the parade and dedication service, the babies are taken back to the nurseries, and the parents return to sit in a section of the auditorium which has been reserved for them. Have this reserved section as near to a door as possible, near the front. Many of the parents will have a difficult time getting their babies back to sleep in the nursery, and will be a little late in getting to the service. Hence, the nearer the reserved section to the door, the less disturbance will be involved as the parents return to the service.

7. *Special Sermon.* The pastor may preach a message on a dedicated child, or some other appropriate sermon in honor of children, trying to reach the parents for Jesus.

HOMECOMING DAY

Homecoming Day is usually conducted in our church on the Thanksgiving weekend to help counterbalance the natural slump of this weekend. Because of the school holidays for this weekend many people will go out of town. However, many, many of them will stay at home and invite their friends and relatives to spend the holidays with them, if there is something special at the church. We have found that our people respond well to days such as this, as they are many times able to reach lost loved ones for Christ in these special services.

1. *Letters.* We mail letters to each of our members, reminding them of Homecoming Day, telling them of the special features for the day, encouraging them to bring friends and relatives. A little artwork helps to add sparkle to the invitation.

2. *Special Letter.* A letter is sent to all former members who can be located, giving them a special invitation to be with us for Homecoming Day. A number of old-timers coming back to the services will more than overcome the loss of those people who go out of town for the weekend; hence, the attendance for the holiday weekend will stay high. There are many former members who would like to spend their holiday weekend visiting the church, if they are invited to a Homecoming Day or special service.

Our Homecoming letter read like this:
The time has come again for our ANNUAL HOME-COMING DAY!! Each year our church family gets together for a great big "dinner on the grounds." THIS SUNDAY, November 27th, is the big day!

We will have our regular Sunday school and preaching service on Sunday morning; then we will go in a body to the Community House in the City Park, where we will all eat lunch together.

After lunch we will return to the auditorium at 3:00 p.m. for a homecoming service. Brother Joe Boyd will bring the homecoming message, and the Singing Spencers will render the special music.

Following is a list of *important items* for YOU to do:
(1) By all means, have your entire family in Sunday school Sunday!
(2) Contact any former members of our church that you know of and invite them to our services!
(3) Plan to BRING YOUR LUNCH and stay with us for the noon meal! DON'T be a "wet blanket" now and go home after the morning service.
(4) If you like, you may take your food to the Community House BEFORE Sunday school. Bring it upstairs where we will have a committee to receive it and arrange it on the tables. If you prefer, you may just bring your lunch with you as you come from the services Sunday morning.
(5) Just to make a complete day of it, plan to come back

to the auditorium at 3:00 o'clock for the homecoming service to hear Brother Boyd and the Spencers!

(6) The *nurseries will be open* for those who want to leave their children 3 years and under until after the homecoming service!

The fellowship here at Miller Road is one of the sweetest in all the world. It will be to your benefit to take advantage of the opportunities of this Sunday. You will have the opportunity to fellowship with former members of our church, members of the Spring Creek Chapel, the Open Door Baptist Church and Eastern Hills Baptist Church (which were missions of our church).

Bring your FRIENDS . . . RELATIVES . . . NEIGH-BORS! EVERYBODY is invited!

T H I S SUNDAY—9:45 a.m.!

3. *Dinner on the Grounds.* For several weeks prior to Homecoming Day our people are reminded of the services, and the "dinner on the grounds." Our own people are encouraged to stay for dinner, and are asked to bring a little extra to take care of our visitors. This is a wonderful time of fellowship.

We have found it advisable in our church to reserve the community house for our lunch in case of rain, cold weather, etc. This also gives a suitable place for the food to be left as the people come to Sunday school if they so desire.

4. *Afternoon Service.* After the "dinner on the grounds" and a time of fellowship, the people come back to the auditorium for an afternoon service. At this service the old-timers are recognized, and other special guests are introduced. A "sing-song" or a "singing" is usually advisable here, followed by a message from some well-known speaker. Testimonies as to what the church has meant to the lives of the people are also in order at this afternoon service, as well as introducing former pastors, etc.

PICTURE TAKING DAY

Picture Taking Day is usually conducted just before Promotion Day each year. August is a good time for this, as the classes will be promoted in a few weeks, and the teachers and pupils will want pictures by which to remember their old classes and departments.

1. *Letters Sent Out.* Letters are mailed to each member of the Sunday school the previous week, reminding them of Picture Taking Day. Be sure to tell why the pictures are being taken—and *when!*—and *where!* Invite the whole family. Following is a copy of one of the letters we have used for this:

We are going to publish a BIG PHOTOGRAPH BOOK entitled "The Miller Road Miracle in Pictures." This book will be much like a high school annual, with pictures and stories all about the Miller Road Baptist Church.

We want YOUR picture to be in this book. The pictures will be taken THIS SUNDAY, August 5th, which has been designated as —

"P I C T U R E   T A K I N G   D A Y"

Picture taking will start promptly at 9:30 Sunday morning — So dress all the children up in their "Sunday best," put on all of the "frills," and be here for this occasion!!

Each CLASS will have its picture made, and each picture will be placed in our new book, which will be published in a few weeks. Copies of this book will be sold all over the country!!

DON'T FORGET . . . Be here *promptly* at 9:30 with ALL the family, as pictures will be taken of *EVERY* person who attends our Sunday school THIS Sunday—from the smallest baby in the nursery—to the oldest Adult!!!

SEE YOU SUNDAY!!

2. *Photographer.* We secure a photographer to take the pictures—a professional photographer, if possible. However, some churches find it advisable to use a member of the church who has a camera and equipment and is good at taking pictures. If the groups are small enough, this can be done easily.

3. *To Create Interest.* In promoting Picture Taking Day a good way to stir interest is to award *free* pictures

to the department or class having the largest percentage of enrollment present. This challenges the teachers, as well as the class members, and results in a significant increase in attendance on this day.

4. *Orders for Pictures.* Announce well in advance the price for the pictures. Orders may be taken for the pictures on the day that they are taken, rather than waiting for proofs, then ordering. Each teacher or departmental superintendent should keep an accurate list of the ones who have ordered pictures, and indicate those who have paid. This list should be kept until all pictures are delivered.

5. *Church Annual.* We have thought it wise before to use these pictures taken on Picture Taking Day, and other pictures taken throughout the year on special occasions, in a church annual—much like a high school annual. This book may be sold to the members for a nominal fee to cover expenses. Former members and other friends might also be interested in such a booklet.

If this is done, by all means take the orders for the annuals before they are ordered by the church. It is a good idea to get the money in advance, also. This way, you will know how many annuals to order.

Picture Taking Day is always fun. All people love to have their pictures taken, and especially like to have them for remembering their classes and departments. This is a successful day each year in our church.

Picture Taking Day may be "stretched out." For example, the Miller Road Baptist Church has grown to such proportions that now we have a special Picture Taking Day for the nursery departments, another for the beginner departments, another for the primaries, another for juniors, another for intermediates and young people, and another for adults. This helps the attendance and creates interest for a number of weeks, rather than just the one Sunday. Too, it is difficult in larger Sunday schools for the photographer to successfully take each class in one Sunday.

If you do have a Picture Taking Day for each group,

rather than taking them all one Sunday, be sure that you send out letters to *each* group the week before they are to have their pictures taken.

Record Breaking Day

This idea can be used effectively almost anywhere. This day may also be advertised and publicized through letters, in your church bulletin or from the pulpit. Get some phonograph records and display them on the platform, or some other conspicuous place in the church—over one write the words "SUNDAY SCHOOL," over another "YOUTH GROUP," over another "OFFERING," and any other church organization that you wish to "break the record." Announce what the previous record attendance is for each one, and then challenge the people to "break the records."

On Record Breaking Sunday, as each goal is reached, the leader of that organization must have the corresponding phonograph record broken over his head. These records are broken at the close of the Sunday school hour, just before the morning service; and at the close of Youth meeting, just prior to the evening service.

Each member will work hard to break all previous records in order to see the phonograph record broken over the superintendent or leader's head.

Absentee Sunday

The general idea here is not to have any absentees in Sunday school on a certain Sunday, but to have *every* member present.

A letter may be sent out to each member with no "T's" in it, because of so many absent T's lately. Also you may want to send out a "T"—either a golf tee, a tea bag, or just a letter "T," asking each person to bring his T to Sunday school so that there will be no absent T.

My dear friend,

We cerxainly are hoping xhax you can be in Sunday school xhis nexx Sunday ax xhe Miller Road Bapxisx

Church. Because of xhe Chrisxmas season and xhe large amounx of sickness, many of our people have been absenx for several Sundays. We wanx xo sxarx xhe New Year wixh a big boom in axxendance xhis Sunday. Plan now xo be in your place. Bring all of xhe children and lex's go over xhe xop for xhe Lord Jesus.

1953 was a banner year for xhe Miller Road Bapxisx Church. Our Sunday school grew by leaps and bounds. We are hoping xhax xhe same xhing can be said ax xhe end of 1954.

By xhe way, I guess xhax by now you are wondering why we have lefx oux all of xhe "T's" in xhis lexxer. THE REASON IS THAT WE HAVE BEEN HAVING SO MANY ABSENT "T's" LATELY, WE JUST DIDN'T HAVE ENOUGH TO USE IN THIS LETTER.

DON'T BE AN ABSENTEE SUNDAY.

Sincerely,
Your Pastor

B-1 Sunday

Get some vitamin B-1, or some tablets containing vitamin B-1 at the drugstore. Send a letter to each member of the Sunday school, enclosing one of the tablets, asking him to take it so he can B-1 in Sunday school the following Sunday. A letter such as the one below creates interest and increases the attendance:

Enclosed you will find a little pill containing Vitamin B-1. Please take this pill so that you can B-1 of 2,000 in Sunday school at the

Miller Road Baptist Church on November 13th . . .

As you know, each year in November we set a "High Attendance Day" as a sort of anniversary of the growth of our church. Two years ago our motto was "From 44 to 444 in one year"; last year it was "From 44 to 1,044 in two years"; this year it is "From 44 to 2,000 in three years"!!

To encourage you to B-1 of this 2,000 on November 13th, the following features have been arranged:

(1) Mrs. Billy Sunday, wife of the famous evangelist of yesteryear, will be our guest and speak to us during the Sunday school hour.

(2) Billy Rosenbaum will sing again! As you know, Brother Billy has been at the point of death for 16 weeks, and has recuperated enough to sing in the quartet for the "Big Day." He will do this even though he is still taking his nourishment through a tube. I know you will want to be here to hear Billy sing!

(3) Another famous quartet will sing! This quartet is known as "The Big Four," composed of Brother and Mrs. Hyles and Brother and Mrs. Keys. They will sing during the opening assembly of the Sunday school!!

(4) A "String Ensemble" composed of four of our church members will play!

(5) A tent will be erected on church property and a Baylor University football player will preach to all the young people at 11:00 a.m. under the tent. He is BILL GLASS, 6 ft., 4 inch, 225 lb. tackle!

(6) During the opening assembly of Sunday school the Singing Spencers will bring us two numbers!

Please, dear friend, take this tablet and B-1 . . . and bring 1 for the

"BIG DAY" on NOVEMBER 13th . . . .

Good Neighbor Sunday

Ask each person to bring a neighbor as his special guest this Sunday. Anyone who brings a neighbor will receive a gift. For example, a nice Bible might be awarded to one who brings as many as ten, or twenty neighbors. A neighbor might be anyone who lives within a fifteen mile radius of the church.

Many good prospects are lined up on Good Neighbor Sunday. Let your members stand and introduce their neighbors in the service.

The sermon topic might be "Who Is My Neighbor?"—

the Good Samaritan story, or some other appropriate sermon.

FRUITFUL FEBRUARY

One of the most successful things that we have ever tried in our church is "Fruitful February." We cut down some medium sized trees and placed them in buckets of dirt, and placed them in the auditorium. One tree was called an "apple tree" to represent the Sunday school, another was a "pear tree" to represent the youth group, and the other was an "orange tree" for the midweek service. We covered the buckets or cans that contained the trees with red, yellow and orange crepe paper.

We mimeographed apples on red, pears on yellow and oranges on orange construction paper. On each apple, pear and orange there was a place indicated for the person to sign his name. These apples, pears and oranges were given to the Sunday school and youth workers to cut out, and it was their job to get everyone *signed up* who would promise to be in Sunday school, the youth meeting, and the midweek service *every* Sunday or Wednesday of the month of February. If they promised to be in Sunday school each Sunday of the month, they became an apple on the apple tree, and so on. These were signed up for each member of the family, and turned back into the office by the workers after they were signed. The apples, pears and oranges were then strung on the trees in the auditorium. It was interesting to see the "trees" fill with fruit as the people signed up to come each Sunday and Wednesday night of the month.

Use of this promotion of Fruitful February should be started four to five weeks early in order to build the attendance for the entire month. This is a workable idea for all age groups.

The people promise to come each Sunday and Wednesday night for an entire month. At the end of the month, most of them, after having been faithful to all of the services for four weeks in a row, have now developed a good habit and will continue to come.

Here is the letter we sent as a reminder:

J U S T   A R R I V E D ! ! !

OUR "ANNUAL" . . .

The "MIRACLE *of* MILLER ROAD *in pictures"* . . .

Many of you have been asking when this book would be ready—As you know, we had previously announced that it would be here Feb. 10th, BUT we are happy to announce that THE BOOK IS NOW READY, and will be available this Sunday, during the Sunday school hour, *February 3rd!!!*

The book contains pictures of the pastor and his family, Brother Harvey, the church staff, the deacons, ALL of our BUILDINGS, and ALL of the pictures of the Sunday school classes and departments that we took on "Picture Taking Day"—*plus* many, many other pictures which you will enjoy and want to keep always. Interesting articles about the history and growth of our church are also contained in this book!! I know that you are ANXIOUS to get this book of "The Miracle of Miller Road" in pictures . . . . FIRST COME, FIRST SERVE . . . This Sunday morning—9:30 a.m.—*February 3rd!!*

A L S O . . . .

This Sunday begins our

"FRUITFUL FEBRUARY"

Have YOU . . . .

> "Put an apple on the apple tree
> for Sunday school all month long —
> A pear on the pear tree says
> you'll be in Training Union with a song . . .
> An orange on the orange tree says we'll
> see you every Wednesday *night!!*
> So, get up a tree for a "FRUITFUL FEBRUARY"
> That's all right!!!

If you have not already "signed up" to be faithful to all of the services of the church, do help us have a "Fruitful February."

Enclosed with this letter you will find an apple which we ask that you sign (you may sign the whole family on this one apple) and BRING IT WITH YOU TO SUNDAY SCHOOL this Sunday.

We are counting on YOU to help us get off to a good start at 9:30 on Sunday morning.

VACATION BIBLE SCHOOL SUNDAY

It is good either at the beginning of vacation Bible school or at the close of it, to have a Sunday honoring vacation Bible school. On this day the workers may be honored, and the children who attended, or who will attend, recognized.

If this special day is held at the close of the school, the work and things accomplished during Bible school might be displayed for a general assembly in the auditorium. Also, the various Bible school characters that are used may appear before the parents. An interesting program in connection with Bible school may be worked out with a little planning. The parents are interested in the things their children do and learn at Bible school, and since many of them never get to work in the school, they do not have an opportunity to see firsthand what goes on at vacation Bible school.

This is good to have during part of the Sunday school hour, and not in the preaching service, as it detracts from the purpose of the service.

CHRISTMAS SUNDAY

A good time to have a special day is on the Sunday nearest Christmas. On this Sunday a small gift of some type might be presented to each member, or to each family attending. We have found a good thing to give is a Scripture text calendar, with the church's name (and perhaps a picture of the church) on it. One year we gave a New Testament to each child present, with the child's name written on it in gold. This is easily done, as you may obtain gold foil from your office supply or art supply store, and the teachers may write the children's names in gold on the Testaments before they are given to the children on the special Sunday.

Some churches permit a "real" Santa Claus to come and present these gifts to the children—other churches with different convictions do not feel it wise.

It seems that since many people go out of town for Christmas anyway, the day should be carefully planned in order to keep the attendance up.

There are many other suggestions which could be given about special days. The ones given here are only to whet your appetite—to help you think of some for yourself. The field is inexhaustible. Literally hundreds have been reached for Christ on these days. God has signally blessed them to His glory, to the saving of sinners, to the edifying of the saved, and to the increased joy of His people.

This chapter is not given to cause conflict in opinions concerning big days. Some will think the above suggestions are too sensational; others will perhaps add even more color to them. Please take what is usable for you, and use it to His glory.

8. Suggestions on How to Promote Big Days

Just to say that we are going to have a big day is not enough. Just a dignified announcement and a few letters is not enough. There must be a definite planned program of promotion. If the big day is successful, then the pastor must lead in the promotion of it from the pulpit. The pastor must first get excited over it, if he is to lead his people to get enthused and to work hard to make the special day a success. Following are some promotion suggestions:

1. *Plan Your Big Days a Year in Advance.* At the beginning of each year I take my calendar and plan the big days. It is sometimes necessary, of course, to make changes during the year; and yet, in order to know the direction that the church is going, and in order to secure speakers for the special occasions, it is good to plan the days far in advance.

2. *Start the Promotion of a Big Day Early.* Start promotion of each big day or special occasion four to six weeks in advance. Announce it from the pulpit at every service. Get excited about it yourself. Stir up the interest in the people at each service for four to six weeks prior to the big day. Your people will not think the day any more important than you do; they will not get any more excited about it than you do. How hard the people work to make the day successful largely depends on how you start promotion of it from the pulpit.

3. *Have Fun as You Prepare for the Big Day.* Churches are so staid in our generation that it seems it would be good for the big days to create freedom of expression. So be sure that the people are in a good frame of mind and are joyful as you look forward to the big day.

4. *Do Not Have a Big Day on a Normal Big Day.* By this I mean that on Easter Sunday your crowds are always good anyway, so it is not wise to have a big day on this Sunday. Have the big days on the difficult Sundays of the year.

5. *Do Not Have a Big Day During a Revival.* A revival, in itself, is something special. Of course, you should strive for a large attendance. By saying do not have a big day I mean this: Do not use your other ideas during a revival, as you will have wasted the ideas. A revival will take care of itself. The spirit runs high during a revival—a special occasion should be when the spirit does not normally run high, in order to level off the church program for the entire year.

6. *Make the Special Occasions Periodic.* One big "record-breaking" day each year is enough. Then, one special occasion each quarter we find to be advisable. Along with these, a special occasion once each month is good. In other words, use one special occasion each month, something *extra* special each three months, and something *super* once each year—which gives a total of sixteen big days each year. Of course, there are other occasions which may be observed throughout the year, but these, I feel, will be enough to keep a church busy and happy.

7. *Do Not Set Too Many Goals.* One or two goals each year is sufficient. It is a bad thing for a church to set a goal and not reach it. It lets the people know that they can fail. Do not ever set a goal unless you are *positively sure* that you can reach it, thereby encouraging the people to set further goals. My suggestion is that goals be set seldom. The *primary* purpose of the big days is not to reach a definite goal, but to reach more people and to create a good spirit among your own people.

8. *When a Goal Is Set, Set It High.* A church will come nearer reaching a high goal than a low one. For example, a church with 150 in Sunday school will come nearer reaching 300 than 200. The people must be chal-

lenged—they will respond to a big challenge more than they will to something that does not tax their energy.

When our church had 44 in Sunday school attendance we set a goal for 173 and had 191. When we had an attendance of 200 in Sunday school we set a goal for 325 and had 339. When we had 300 in Sunday school, we set a goal for 444 and had 618. When we had 450 in Sunday school attendance we set a goal for 666 and had 952. When we had 700 in Sunday school, we set a goal for 1,080 and had 1,181. When we had around 750 to 800 in attendance, we set a goal for 1,300 and had 1,601. Since we have been having 1,000 and over in attendance, we have set goals of 2,000 and had 2,212—and a goal of 3,000 and had 3,163. Something *big* challenges people. The bigness of the challenge will encourage the people to bring their friends and relatives.

9. *Sign Up Methods.* It is sometimes good to use sign up methods, such as bananas to be "one of the bunch," or a link in a chain, or some similar idea. This is good occasionally; however, it can be over used. Perhaps once each year is enough for a sign up method. A sign up method seems to do more in a revival effort than at any other time, because the pastor has each night of the meeting to ask people to sign up and promise to come.

10. *Get Your People to Bring Their Friends and Relatives.* Suggest that the members bring their relatives from out of town for the big day, or friends from a neighboring city, or anyone who can come from churches that are not real soul winning, Bible preaching churches. There are a number of things that getting people from out of town will do, though it will not build your own church immediately: Many of them will be saved. People who live outside your city are just as much in need of Christ as those who live in your city. Many of them will come with relatives for a big occasion and be converted.

It will help the people who come so that they will go back and encourage their own churches to be on fire for God. Many times just one person who is encouraged in a special service in your church can go back to his own church and ignite a flame that will burn in soul winning zeal for months to come.

It will bring publicity to your church. Every church needs publicity. If your city is one of any size, almost everyone has friends and is constantly meeting people who live close enough to be reached by your church; hence, it is a good way to build for the future.

Many people are in liberal churches which do not believe in the new birth. They need to be taken from these churches. Their attendance at your church on a big day may make them dissatisfied with their liberal church, so that they will return home and place their membership in a church that believes in the new birth, soul winning, and other basic Christian beliefs.

On an extra special day people from three or four states and scores of other towns come to visit the services. Put special emphasis on making it a "family affair" and many will come to be reunited with loved ones.

At each service for four or five weeks prior to the big day, ask for a show of hands of people who have already gotten promises. Find out how many promises you have. Give special attention to those who have already gotten people to promise to come with them. It is a good idea to spend at least five minutes at each public service in the promotion of the big day.

11. *Build Your Big Days around the Pastor.* If you build your big days around visiting speakers, then people will not see the church in a normal service. They will come and enjoy the visiting speaker, go back home and wish they could go to a church like that all of the time. Then, the next Sunday they will come to hear you, perhaps. The special occasion is over; you are back to normal—the prospects are not there, the souls do not walk the aisles in good number as they did previously on the big day. The people think it is the preaching of the visiting speaker that did it, and that the pastor is not as capable. Hence, they will not come back.

However, if they come on a big occasion and hear your pastor and feel the spirit and see the souls saved, they will realize they can see that every Sunday, and will want to come back and hear the pastor regularly. Be sure that the pastor is the speaker on big occasions.

12. *Make Much Use of the Mail.* The week prior to the big day, after it has been announced and publicized in the public church services, send out letters publicizing the special day. Sometimes we send out two letters in one week—one at the first of the week, another later in the week. Or, a letter at the first of the week and a postal card later in the week is good. These are sent out to each member enrolled in our Sunday school most of the time—which means that each member of the family will get a letter. The second letter sent out the same week might be sent out to the church roll, one letter to each family.

9. Some Practical Pointers Concerning the Sunday School

The life's blood of any church is in the Sunday school. This teaching period of the Word of God is vitally important to all New Testament churches. The twentieth century church is built around its Sunday school. When someone wants to know the size of a church, he immediately asks what the Sunday school attendance is. The preaching service attendance, youth groups attendance and midweek service attendance depend largely upon the Sunday school. If this is true, then our Sunday school must be important. Below are some pointers and suggestions for the Sunday school.

1. *The Enlistment of Workers.* In order to have the proper kind of meal, there must be the proper kind of cook. To have the proper kind of cars, there must be the proper kind of mechanics. It is important to choose carefully the teachers for the Sunday school.

Election. Teachers should be elected by the church once each year; however, no teacher should be chosen in the church unless previously approved by the pastor. The pastor should have the right to approve or disapprove each worker in the church.

Training Course. At the beginning of each year, immediately following the election of teachers and officers, a course in teaching should be offered. It is good to have such a course on the first of October each year, if your new church year begins on October first. One suggestion for such a course is to have the pastor teach the adult workers, and perhaps include young people's and intermediate teachers. Then, have some junior specialist teach the junior workers, and then have a special course for the elementary workers, giving instruction for four or five nights to all of those who will lead the Sunday school for the new year.

Check List. Some churches use pledge cards, but through the years I have tried to stay away from the signing of any kind of pledges; however, we do ask our workers to do several things, and present them with a check list so they may see whether or not they are doing the things expected. The following is a check list we use with our workers:

WHAT KIND OF TEACHER AM I?

1. Do I live a separated life?
2. Do I have a daily private devotion?
3. Is my thought life pure?
4. Do I start studying my lesson on Monday?
5. Do I have the right motives? (love for my pupils)
6. Am I prepared physically to teach?
7. Am I prepared mentally to teach?
8. Am I prepared spiritually to teach?
9. Do I pray daily for each pupil?
10. Have I visited in the home of each pupil this quarter?
11. Do I visit all of my absentees?
12. Am I a pastor to my pupils?
13. Do I attend teacher's meeting?
14. Do I support the entire church program?
15. Am I faithful?
16. When I am absent, do I contact my superintendent by Wednesday night?
17. Have I had a monthly class meeting?
18. Is my class properly organized?
19. Do I get up early enough on Sunday mornings?
20. Do I "brush over" my lesson again on Sunday mornings?
21. Do I make my classroom attractive?
22. Do I greet my class members as they come in?
23. Do I meet any visitors before class?

24. Are my visitors properly introduced in class?
25. Do I enlist any new members?
26. Does my class spend a maximum of five minutes on announcements and business?
27. Do I get all visitors to properly fill out visitors' slips?
28. Do I tithe?
29. Do I leave my quarterly at home?
30. Do I teach only from the Bible?
31. Do I remember not to make any pupil read or talk?
32. Do I have an interest getter for my lesson?
33. Do I have a written aim?
34. Am I the right age for my pupils?
35. Do I stay on the subject?
36. Do I teach until the bell rings?
37. Do I go from class straight to the auditorium?
38. Do I sit with the lost, if I have any in my class?
39. Do I keep the Lord's Day holy?
40. Is my class of utmost importance in my life?

Dismissal of Workers. When a worker's life becomes contrary to the teachings of the church morally, then it is the duty of the pastor, or some leader, to go to him and ask him to resign his position. This may be done tactfully sometimes; other times it must be done frankly and candidly. It is better to lose the worker than to pollute the Sunday school and rob the church of its needed power.

Elementary Program Planning. One person should be enlisted to be in charge of the elementary work of the Sunday school. Each group of workers in the various departments should have a monthly planning meeting. This meeting is apart from the regular weekly officers' and teachers' meeting. All of the primary workers should have a meeting to plan their work; the same is true with beginner and the nursery workers. At these meetings they may discuss their problems and plan their handwork and interest centers for the coming month.

2. *Weekly Officers and Teachers' Meeting.* The weekly officers' and teachers' meeting may be conducted forty-five minutes preceding the midweek service. A good time is from seven o'clock to seven forty-five.

In our church the first twenty minutes of the meeting are devoted to promotion, planning, looking forward to big days and discussing the various problems of the workers. The last twenty-five minutes are devoted to teaching the Sunday school lesson. The pastor teaches the lesson. He has a mimeographed outline of the lesson, as he interprets it, then teaches it to the teachers on Wednesday night. This has proven helpful in many Sunday schools.

There is no weekly departmental teachers' meeting. This is taken care of by the departments themselves as they feel the need. Most of our departments have a monthly planning meeting where they plan their work for each month. This is good, especially when it is spontaneous and carried out by the workers.

3. *Division of Departments and Classes.* It is good to have a graded Sunday school. By this I mean have the classes divided by ages. Following are some suggestions as to division of classes:

According to Number of Qualified Teachers. Many suggest that adult classes should be divided into groups of fifteen to twenty-five each. However, many churches do not have enough qualified adult teachers to divide the classes into small groups. It is better to have just one large class if only one qualified teacher is available. However, if you have more teachers who are qualified, then more classes may be made. The classes should not be too large—or too small. The enrollment of the adult classes here in the Miller Road Baptist Church varies from 30 to 80, with an average attendance in each class of approximately 20 to 25. This seems practical—there are enough in each class to make it interesting, yet it is small enough to care for the needs of each member individually.

According to Facilities. Many churches do not have the facilities that other churches do; hence, the classes must be smaller in some cases. If the classrooms are smaller, have smaller classes. The church must be adapted to its buildings, and to each situation. One of the greatest mistakes being made today is the idea that all churches should be alike and that every situation is the same. This is not true. Some churches may find it wise to have large classes; others, to have smaller ones. No two churches have the same field, the same opportunities, the same possibilities, the same likes and dislikes, or the same constituency. Each church must adapt its division of classes to its own local situation.

Division of Elementary Groups. In our elementary groups, of course, we have the nurseries, beginners and primaries. The number of departments or classes that you have in each group, of course, would depend upon the number of children. However, we do suggest that you have at least one separate department for each of the above three groups—nursery is composed of those through age three; beginners are the four- and five-year-old children, and the primaries are ages six through eight. If you have enough children it is good to have a department for each year—for example, one for the six-year-olds, one for the seven-year-old pupils, and on. If at all possible, never mix the preschool age children with those who are already attending public school, as their abilities and attention span are not the same.

4. *Sunday School Helps.* There are many quarterlies and many commentaries that can help the teachers. Although any teacher may secure a copy of any teaching literature he needs, we have found it best through the years to use the following:

We provide all of our adult teachers with the *Bible Expositor and Illuminator.* For the most part, this is a good help. The teachers in our church are favorable in their comments on it. This may be secured from the Union Gospel Press, Cleveland, Ohio.

The pastor presents a mimeographed outline to his workers each week. In preparing this outline the pastor does not use any help but the Bible. It is his own interpretation of the lesson from the Bible.

The teacher should make his own outline for Sunday, and study his lesson apart from outside helps, asking God to lead him to the truths of the Scripture.

There are other good helps such as *Higley's Bible Commentary*, *Peloubet's Commentary*, and others.

It is always good to have a Bible dictionary and a concordance. These are two of the finest helps that a teacher can have.

10. Training Union or Youth Group Suggestions

One of the most difficult services in which to build attendance and create interest is in the training union or youth hour. This hour usually is each Sunday evening, just preceding the evening worship service. It can be a definite help to a church, if properly operated, in the building of the spirit and attendance of the Sunday night service, and also in the training of the church members. Several suggestions are given here to help in providing effective Sunday evening meetings:

1. *Church-Wide Appointment of All Officers.* Most groups elect their own officers. In many cases they elect new officers each three months. It has been found wise in some churches to have the officers—such as presidents, vice-presidents, group captains, Bible quiz leaders, etc., elected by the church, and hold a church-elected office for one year. This may make the people feel that their job is more important, and it may cease to be just pushing an office off on someone who did not have the resistance to say "no."

2. *The Pastor Should Approve the Lesson.* Each week the pastor should review the program in the quarterly. If it is advisable to use it, well and good. If not, he should see that the group has one which will be helpful —either prepare one of his own, or find another one. No quarterly is perfect, and since the pastor is accountable for what the people receive in his church, he should be careful to scan the material used. If it is good, use it. If not, prepare something else in its place. This is done each week in our church.

3. *Weekly Planning Meetings.* At the Miller Baptist

Church a weekly training union program planning meeting is conducted at six o'clock on Sunday evening. The program is planned for the following Sunday. A new idea is presented each week at this meeting to help the leaders in the presentation of their program. A Bible drill suggestion is also given each week. Just a giving of the parts is not enough. A unique and unusual way to present the program for the following week is given each Sunday evening. Also, at this meeting problems are discussed and necessary adjustment made. It is a helpful meeting for presidents, vice-presidents, group captains and Bible drill leaders in adult, young people and intermediate groups.

4. *Elementary Work.* The elementary groups in our church use the Gardner System. This literature and work books may be found at most book stores. This work is headed by an elementary director, who oversees all of the work of the nursery, beginner and primary departments. The elementary director has a monthly planning meeting on the last Sunday afternoon in each month. At this meeting the director passes out our mimeographed planning sheets, which give suggestions for presenting each program for the month, along with interest center suggestions and samples, handwork patterns and Bible drill suggestions. Samples of the program material, handwork and interest centers are displayed for each program for the benefit of the workers. This is a splendid method, and God has certainly used it to bless the hearts of our boys and girls.

5. *Junior Work.* Our junior groups also have a director who meets with the leaders and directors of each junior group once each month to plan their programs and work. The junior director also has mimeographed planning sheets for the workers, along with mimeographed Bible drill suggestions and patterns and attendance reminders. At these meetings the workers in each group may exchange ideas on how to present their programs to make them more helpful and interesting.

11. Vacation Bible School at Miller Road

By JO STRICKLAND, *Pastor's Secretary*

During the past two or three years we have had many requests for information regarding our vacation Bible schools. We have tried to help some pastors and churches by conducting short Bible school clinics. After our clinic last year we were requested by a number of pastors and workers to put our ideas and suggestions in print. We have prepared this chapter in the hope that it will be of some help to you in planning your vacation Bible school.

I believe that the key to a successful Bible school, to having one that both the pupils and workers will enjoy and be blessed from, is *advance planning*. Advance planning makes a great deal of difference in what actually goes on during the week or two weeks that your school is conducted.

1. *Set Your Date Early*. Early in the year, as the pastor plans his annual program or schedule, the vacation Bible school should be considered and a definite date set for it. Most churches find that June is the most acceptable month for it—but there are some churches which wait until August, just before school starts again. We think that June is a good time; however, we do not prefer the *first* week after school is out for the summer. True, many children go on vacations as soon as school is out; but usually the children respond much better if the school is not conducted until they have been out of public school for at least a couple of weeks.

Many churches have a two-week school, others prefer ten days, and still others have found it advisable to have school only one week. We have found that the latter works best for us. It seems that with so much time and work involved, the workers give their best for a one week school; but many of them cannot give themselves completely to a two-week schedule. If preparation day and enrollment is held in advance, perhaps on Friday or Saturday before the school is to begin on Monday, then much can be accomplished in a five-day school.

2. *Publicize Your Bible School.* For several weeks prior to the date that your Bible school is to begin, publicize the school. This may be done in the church bulletin or newspaper, through the Sunday school classes and departments, through the mail, and from the pulpit. Your pastor can do more for you in publicizing your school than anyone else. The response of the children who attend, and the workers who help with the school, largely depends on how interested the pastor becomes in it, and how excited he gets about it himself as he announces it from the pulpit.

3. *Enlistment of Workers.* As soon as possible after the date has been set for the school, enlist your superintendent of the school. Many times the pastor serves as superintendent of the school, or perhaps the associate pastor or educational director fills this position. If someone other than the pastor is superintendent, then he, of course, will work closely with the pastor in planning the school.

The school superintendent may wish to enlist *all* of the workers, or he may prefer only to enlist the various departmental superintendents, and then assist them in enlisting the workers for their own departments. It is good to use as many workers as possible with the same age groups that they teach in Sunday school or youth groups. This way they are already acquainted with most of the pupils who will attend, with their problems and abilities. This makes it better not only for the workers, but for the pupils as well. In addition to the teachers and workers in the Sunday school and youth groups, others should also be used. This is a wonderful time to train new workers for the Sunday school and youth groups. Many of the Sunday workers have secular jobs and are unable to help in Bible school while, at the same time, there are many mothers and housewives who are willing to work in Bible school who feel they cannot teach on Sundays. Therefore, Bible school time is a good time for training new workers.

4. *Departmental Divisions.* The more departments you have, the greater Bible school attendance you will have. If at all possible, have at least one department for each age group—that is, one for those under four years of age, one for those four and five, one for those six, seven and eight, one for the juniors—nine through twelve, and one for those thirteen and up. If your school is a large one, it is our suggestion that you have a department for each year—one for the six-year-olds, one for the seven-year-olds, etc. At any rate, try to keep the preschool age children from those who go to school, because of the difference in their attention span and abilities. You will find it helpful if you can have a *department* for about every twenty-five or thirty pupils, and a *worker* for every five pupils.

5. *Planning Meetings.* Textbooks that are to be used in the school should be given to the superintendents of departments as early as possible, so that they may study them and decide upon the lessons or programs which they are to use. Then, as soon as the superintendents have had the opportunity to study the textbooks, each departmental superintendent should get together with the workers of the department, for a planning meeting.

We have found it helpful to have a general meeting with the school superintendent, pastor, and *all* workers twice before the school begins—the first time in the beginning of the planning of the Bible school, then again the week before the school is to start. This way general plans may be discussed and questions answered at the first meeting. At the second meeting, a check may be made to see if everything is ready and in order for the beginning of the school. Between these two general meetings, the department heads will probably need to have at least two meetings with their workers to make individual departmental plans.

Textbooks should be given out and planning started five to six weeks before time for the Bible school to begin.

If the work for each day is carefully planned, all mimeographing done, supplies bought, and the work for the entire week presented to the workers in advance, the Bible school will run smoothly, the workers will enjoy it and be blessed by it and the pupils will greatly benefit from the school.

More about individual lesson planning will be said later in this chapter.

6. *Preparation Day and Parade.* On Friday or Saturday morning before the school is to begin on Monday, it is helpful to have Preparation day, and if possible, a parade.

The children may come at the time that Bible school will begin each day—line up and march into the auditorium, where they will be given brief instructions about the procedure for the school, to be followed each day the following week. They may be told where each department will meet, and leave the auditorium by department. Each group may go to its department for pre--enrollment.

As much of the enrolling as possible should be done on preparation day. This will save much valuable time, and cause less confusion on the first day of the school.

We have found it helpful to do some pre-enrollment through the Sunday school departments prior to the first day of Bible school. This is especially helpful and saves much time in the preschool age departments where the children cannot write and many do not know their birthdays or addresses.

After pre-enrollment is completed in the departments —then it is time for the parade! This is always exciting and fun for the children, and the publicity helps the Bible school attendance. Each car in the parade may be decorated with posters or banners, giving the time and place of the Bible school. You may also wish to have circulars printed to be thrown from the cars as they travel. Some kind of public address or loudspeaker system is helpful for announcements about the Bible school as the parade progresses. Plans for this should be taken into consideration well in advance.

7. *Daily Time Schedule for the School.* A daily time schedule is important if the school is to operate smoothly. Each departmental superintendent should have a tentative time schedule worked out in advance, with a copy for each worker in the department. Some schools meet for three hours each day; some for two and one-half hours each day. For a one-week school, I think it is good if the school lasts for three hours each day; for a ten-day or two-week school, I believe that two and one-half hours daily is ample time.

Following is a suggested time schedule designed for one of our beginner groups, which might be helpful in working out one of your own. Of course, each age group would vary, since the older groups would have longer Bible study, mission activity, and more extensive notebook work.

Suggested Time Schedule for Beginners
Monday through *Friday:* 9:00 - 11:30 a.m.
(*Preparation day*—pre-enrollment and parade
on Friday, June 8th)

Approximate Time:

9:00 a.m.—Line up by departments and march into auditorium

9:00—9:20 a.m.—General assembly in auditorium

In Your Department:

First 5 Minutes—(If you have a piano in your department, have pianist there playing as the children come to the department. This will aid in getting the children settled.)

Explain about the mission offering that will be taken each day and tell where it will go. Then take the offering first so children will not lose their money.

10 Minutes—Go to tables (assign children to same teacher and same table for each day of the school). Workers at tables assist department secretary in checking

records, filling out enrollment cards on new members each day.

Mark attendance charts. Stick on stars, seals (if you use individual attendance charts, be sure each child has one with his name on it).

15 Minutes—Come back to large group (all departments together).

Have songs selected and planned in advance to go with lesson.

Fingerplays or relaxation exercises.

Bible story for the day. Prayer. (Use flannelgraph, or other interest center with Bible story.)

20 Minutes—After the Bible story, go back to tables. Memory verse for the day to be used or taught by teachers (may have poster for this). Then, begin notebook work (one page each day) until time for refreshments.

10 Minutes—Refreshments. Have thanks in your department before going outside. Instruct children to return to department promptly after refreshments.

10 Minutes—If notebook work was not completed before refreshments, come back to tables and finish work. Be sure each child's name is on his notebook cover, and on each *page,* if a page is added each day of the school.

10 Minutes—The whole department meets together for a child life or conduct story. If you do not have a conduct story for each day, you may use action songs here, not above with your Bible story time. Also fingerplays relaxation exercises may be used here.

20 Minutes—Return to auditorium for fun time with "Silly Billy," "Ole Timer" and "Phooidini." (If necessary, one or two workers may remain in the department to straighten up and get ready for the next work.)

25 Minutes—Handwork. Let the children make something each day. Plan handwork that has teaching value, to help accomplish purpose for the day.

Let the children do as much of the work as possible. Don't do it for them. Plan your handwork to be simple enough that they may enjoy doing it. Don't plan so much that they will have to be rushed to finish what they are supposed to do for the day.

5 Minutes—Clean up time and announcements. Try to finish your work in time for the children to help clean tables. Superintendent should give the teachers about five minutes "warning" before clean-up time so that they may complete their work for the day. Avoid rush and confusion these last few minutes. Keep the children orderly.

Workers should be sure to keep younger children inside the rooms until they are called for. Be careful that none of the pupils get lost or upset.

Each day right after refreshments, you may let the children get drinks and go to the restroom. This will avoid children running in and out during the sessions each day.

After school each day teachers should remain for five minutes to review the schedule for the following day with the superintendent, to check to see that each worker has enough supplies, etc. Be sure that each worker understands what the plans are for each day.

At least one worker from each department should be assigned to come early each day (a different one each day) to help the children who come first know where to line up. This will avoid confusion among the younger children before school ever begins, and is helpful throughout the day.

This schedule is merely a guide to help you in adjusting to your own schedule. Do not try to pack too much into one day. If you find that you have too much work planned for any one day, leave some of it off. If on other days you find that you have some extra time, you should have some games, puzzles, modeling clay and other activities planned in advance for "fill-in" activity.

After your time schedule is worked out, it is easier to plan your program for each day, since you will then know approximately how much time you may use for each activity. Each *worker* in your department should be given a copy of this schedule.

Now, it is time for the department superintendent, along with the "right-hand man" or associate superintendent, to get together with all of the workers to plan the lesson and activities for each day. The following planning sheet might be helpful to you in working out your Bible school programs:

Daily Lesson Plans for Beginners

Unit for the Week: "Learning about Homes"

(You may also wish to insert your aim or purpose for the week, or you may wish to include a purpose or aim for each day).

Monday

Lesson Title: "What Makes a Happy Home?"

Aim: Lead the children to work out the answer to the above question—through their work, through their play, conversation, the Bible story, the handwork, etc.

Bible Story: Exodus 1:7; 2:10—"How Miriam Helped to Make Her Home Happy" (Use Baby Moses Flannelgraph)

Conduct or Child Life Story: Page 26 of textbook—"Mary Finds out What Makes a Happy Home"

Bible Verse for Today: "Let us love one another." (I John 4:7. (To be on feather of colored construction paper—pasted on "chief" on memory verse poster—one poster for each table.)

Notebook: Start notebook today. The back is mimeographed on green construction paper, in shape of a home. Put the child's name on page 1 in place indicated. Use page 2 to stick on flag seals, pledges, Bible, etc. (This may be done on Tuesday, or whenever you have time.)

Page for notebook for today is picture of a home (this may be child's own home, or picture of a home from magazine—teachers will have these.)

Handwork: House—mimeographed on white construction paper. Teachers will have them cut out in advance,

Children may put them together, so that they stand up. (They may take these home.)

Other Suggestions for Monday:

Supplies That I Will Need for Monday:

.... is to come early on Monday
        (Name of worker)

to greet children who come early, and assist them in lining up.

Tuesday

Lesson Title: "I Can Talk to God in My Home"

Aim: To let the children know that they can talk to God any time, anywhere, as they would talk to a friend. Try to make prayer a happy experience for them.

Bible Story

Conduct or Child Life Story: "How Bobby Learned to Talk to God in His Own Home" (Page 31 of textbook)

Bible Verse for Today: "God will hear me." Micah 7:7. (Mimeographed on colored paper—cut out and paste on poster.)

Notebook: Put in page with picture of family praying— children may color picture. The Family Fingers' Good Morning finger play may be pasted on back of page 1. Also, paste the pledges, flags and Bible seals on today if this was not done yesterday.

Handwork: Plaque of boy and girl praying, on black construction paper, spatter painted, with gummed hanger on back. (You will need cigar box, screen wire, white shoe polish, old toothbrushs for spatter painting.)

Other Suggestions and Materials for Tuesday:

.... is to come early on Tuesday
        (Name of worker)

to greet children.

Wednesday

Lesson Title: "God Teaches Birds and Animals to Make Homes"

Bible Story: Part of the creation story—Genesis 1. (Use flannelgraph.) Other Scripture references: Matthew 6:26, 8:20; Luke 12:6; Deuteronomy 32:11; Job 37:8; Psalm 84:3; 104:10-12, 16-18.

Conduct or Child Life Story: "How the Birds Made a Home"

Bible Verse for Today: "Your heavenly Father feedeth them." Matthew 6:26.

"The birds . . . have nests." Matthew 8:20.

Notebook: Teachers should have the bird's nests (on brown construction paper) cut out. Also, have the eggs cut out of white or light blue. Let the children paste the bird nests on their notebook pages, then paste eggs in nests and stick on bird seals.

Handwork: Teachers should have fish cut out of white construction paper. Let children cover with glitter or Christmas snow. Tie string through mouth. Wheel of "Animal Friends." Let children stick animal seals on lower circle. Have hole cut in top circle, brad in center. As they turn top circle, animals will show through hole.

Other Suggestions for Wednesday: For special interest centers, have one teacher bring bowl of goldfish, someone else a real bird's nest, a real bird or other animal.

.... is to come early on Wednesday
        (Name of worker)
    to greet children.

Thursday

Lesson Title: "We Think and Talk about Church Homes"

Aim: Teach the children the name of their church and of their pastor. Lead them to feel that it is "their" church home; also, let them know that it is God's house.

Bible Story: Use flannelgraph of Samuel.

Conduct or Child Life Story: 'How Some Children Helped in God's House"

Bible Verse for Today: "I was glad when they said unto me, Let us go into the house of the Lord." Psalm 122:1.

Notebook: Let the children paste a picture of a church (or of their own church) on the notebook page for today. Perhaps they will want to stick on seals of boys and girls going to church.

Handwork: Teachers will have church cut out of white construction paper, with windows cut out. Let children paste colored cellophane paper across the back to look like light shining through the windows. They may also paste artificial "grass" around the church, and stick flower seals on.

Other Suggestions for Today: Plan some kind of note or reminder to send home to parents, inviting them to visit the school on Friday, if that is the last day of the school. Also, tell them about the picnic plans, if there is to be one.

.... is to come early on Thursday
        (Name of worker)
    to greet children.

Friday

Lesson Title: "We Talk about Jesus and the Heavenly Home"

Bible Story: The Heavenly Home

Bible Verse for Today: "I go to prepare a place for you." John 14:2b.

Notebook: Finish notebook today so that children may take it home. The page for today is: Church window that opens; let children paste Sallman's head of Christ seal inside window. Look through the notebook with the children, reviewing each lesson briefly, and the Bible verses that have been used.

Let the children take home any work that they have not taken during the week; also, let them take their attendance charts. (This plan is based on a five day school.)

Suggestion for attendance: You may have crowns with five points cut out of blue (or any color) construction paper. Let child paste a gold or silver star on one point each day he is present. Have child's name printed on crown in white or gold ink. Punch hole in each side and run rubber band through it. The children may wear these crowns at commencement, if you have one. If not, let them wear them home on the last day of the school.

If there is to be a commencement program, keep a sample of the notebook and of each piece of work that you have made during Bible school for display.

The ideas for handwork, mission projects and interest centers for the various age groups are unlimited. We try to plan handwork with teaching value, or try to make something which may be useful either at home or around the church—for example, some of the older students make pulpit stands for the classrooms, coat racks, hat trees, planters for the windows or tables, curtains, aprons for the nursery and beginner children to wear while pasting, etc.

With some study and planning, some interesting notebooks, maps and other items may be made in mission study with the older pupils.

We trust that the foregoing sample daily lesson plans will help you in making your plans for your own group.

Some General Suggestions for Bible School

The Pastor's Part in Bible School. Vacation Bible school time is a wonderful time for the children to get to know the pastor, and for the pastor, in turn, to become acquainted with the children. Many of the children who come to Sunday school, whose parents do not attend the church, never get to stay for the preaching services, and do not even know the pastor. Our pastor takes an active part in our Bible schools. He and the children look forward to this time each year, when the pastor will spend some time with the children. He usually dresses informally during the days of Bible school and drops by several departments each day, just to "stick his head in" for a moment to visit. Then, as the department comes out for refreshments, he goes out and visits with them during refreshment time. Later in this chapter we will mention the pastor's part in the general assembly of the Bible school in the auditorium.

We have special Bible school "characters" each year, which we shall discuss later in this chapter. The pastor publicizes these characters from the pulpit each service for several weeks before the school begins. It seems that the pastor's interest and excitement about the school, and the way he creates enthusiasm about it from the pulpit, do more than anything else in helping us have the large numbers that we do have in our school each year. For the past few years we have had an enrollment of near 1,000 with an average attendance of nearly 700!

Special Events in Our Bible School. Many schools only have one general assembly of the school in the auditorium, which is the first fifteen or twenty minutes each morning. However, we have two sessions in the auditorium for the entire school—the first one as soon as the children arrive in the morning, as they line up and march into the auditorium, and then again later in the morning, usually about forty-five minutes before the close of school each day.

At this first session in the auditorium we have the usual procedure, with pledges to the flags and the Bible; then, we use the second assembly for our special events. This is the highlight of our school, and we perhaps reach more boys and girls for our Bible school through promotion of these characters and events than by any other method.

Each year we have "Silly Billy," the ugliest boy in the world; "Phooidini," the gospel magician; and "The Ole Timer," who is Silly Billy's grandfather. The pastor presents each of these characters when we are in the auditorium the second time. "Silly Billy" and "Ole Timer" is an ad-lib affair with the pastor. It is difficult to put into words just how effective this skit is each day. Then Phooidini, the magician, presents a gospel "trick," which the children all look forward to each day. Each of these "characters" wears some kind of costume, which may be rented for a nominal price at any costume shop, or you may make one of your own which will be just as effective. The "magician" may get various games or tricks, from a hobby or novelty shop.

Crowning the "King and Queen." Another thing that all of the children, as well as the workers, look forward to each day, is the crowning of the king and queen. It is announced in advance, and each morning of the school, that each girl who brings the most visitors to Bible school who do not attend our Sunday school, will be crowned "queen for the day." The boy who brings the most visitors that do not attend our Sunday school will be crowned "king for the day." The king and queen for the day are determined as we come into the auditorium the second time, after the records have been completed, and they are crowned at the beginning of this second assembly, and sit on the platform with their crowns on during this second session. Each day the king and queen get to keep their crown to take home with them. (These crowns are made by some of the workers from white poster paper and silver glitter.) At the close of the school we find out which boy and girl have brought the most visitors for the entire school, and they are crowned king and queen of the Bible school. Their pictures are taken, and usually used in our church newspaper.

The Mission Offering. Before the Bible school begins, we decide where our mission offering will go. The children get more joy from bringing their money each day if they know exactly where it is going. It also helps the departmental superintendents in planning their mission activities and interest centers. We send our mission offering each year to some of our own missionaries who have gone out from our church, and whom the children and the workers know.

This mission offering is taken in the departments each morning. A report of approximately how much money is received in each department is turned in with the records each day. Then, when we are in the auditorium the second time, the pastor gives a report of the offering. We have a large balloon, usually in the shape of some animal. The pastor has to put a big "puff" into the balloon for each dollar received in the mission offering. As the offering increases each day, the balloon gets larger and larger. There is much fun and excitement as the children wait for the balloon to burst in the pastor's face.

Many times the offering increases so rapidly that two or three balloons are burst before the end of Bible school.

Commencement. We have found it advisable in recent years not to have a commencement program at the close of Bible school because of the size of our school. By the time each department had just a few minutes on the program, it would run in to quite a lengthy program, and the children, as well as the parents, become restless. Also, when there is such a large number of pupils, it is difficult to have "open house" in the departments following the commencement because of limited space.

However, if your school is small, it is good to have commencement. Members of each department may be given a few moments to present some of their work and the things they have learned, at a general assembly in the auditorium. Diplomas may be presented by the pastor or the school superintendent as each department finishes its part in the program.

One year we had our commencement on Sunday morning following the close of Bible school on Friday. This was publicized as Bible School Sunday. At the beginning of the Sunday school hour, everyone assembled in the auditorium. The children went through the regular Bible school procedure, repeating the pledges, etc. Then the various "characters" are presented and the king and queen crowned. The Bible school workers are introduced, and each department has a display on the platform, or some place in the auditorium, showing some of the work done during the week.

We have also found it advisable to invite the parents to visit the various departments sometime during the school, perhaps on the last day of the school.

Vacation Bible school can mean much to your Sunday school and to your church, and can be a time of enjoyment rather than a drudgery if it is well planned. Although we do not have a decision service each day in which the children are pressed to make a decision for Christ, we do have a time during our school when the pastor speaks to the juniors in a special service, presents the plan of salvation and gives them an opportunity to be saved. Each child who comes forward to accept Christ is dealt with separately by the pastor and associate pastor, and the Lord has blessed us each year with a number of genuine conversion experiences in our Bible schools. As a result of these experiences, many of the parents have been reached for Christ.

We believe it well worth your efforts to have a vacation Bible school in your church each summer, and we trust that some of the foregoing outlines and suggestions will be of help to you in planning your school.